BECOMING AN ADULT

T0182258

BECOMING AN ADULT

advice on
taking control &
living a happy,
meaningful life

DR. HENRY CLOUD

ZONDERVAN
BOOKS

Zondervan Books

Becoming an Adult

Portions of this book were excerpted and adapted from *Changes That Heal* (9780310351788).

Published in Grand Rapids, Michigan, by Zondervan. Zondervan is a registered trademark of The Zondervan Corporation, L.L.C., a wholly owned subsidiary of HarperCollins Christian Publishing, Inc.

Requests for information should be addressed to customercare@harpercollins.com.

All Scripture quotations, unless otherwise indicated, are taken from The Holy Bible, New International Version®, NIV®. Copyright © 1973, 1978, 1984, 2011 by Biblica, Inc.® Used by permission of Zondervan. All rights reserved worldwide. www.Zondervan. com. The "NIV" and "New International Version" are trademarks registered in the United States Patent and Trademark Office by Biblica, Inc.®

Scripture quotations marked NASB are taken from the *New American Standard Bible*®, Copyright © 1960, 1962, 1963, 1968, 1971, 1972, 1973, 1975, 1977, 1995 by The Lockman Foundation. Used by permission. (www.Lockman.org)

Any Internet addresses (websites, blogs, etc.) and telephone numbers in this book are offered as a resource. They are not intended in any way to be or imply an endorsement by Zondervan, nor does Zondervan vouch for the content of these sites and numbers for the life of this book.

Published in association with Yates & Yates, www.yates2.com.

Cover design: Jamie DeBruyn
Interior design: Kait Lamphere

ISBN 978-0-310-16116-5 (softcover)
ISBN 978-0-310-16117-2 (eBook)
ISBN 978-0-310-16118-9 (audiobook)

Library of Congress Control Number: 2024009667

Printed in the United States of America

24 25 26 27 28 LBC 5 4 3 2 1

CONTENTS

ACKNOWLEDGMENTS

I did not set out to write *Changes That Heal*, the original book that inspired *Becoming an Adult*. It was the product of a lot of people, without whose input this book would not exist. The ideas here are composites of many experiences over many years that involve faithful servants of Jesus Christ, and I would like to acknowledge some of the persons specifically.

Dr. John Townsend, my friend and associate, has been instrumental in the development of the model presented here. Through many hours of dialogue and team teaching, his input and thinking have added much to my understanding of Scripture and of emotional life. I am indebted to him for the loyalty of his friendship, the discipline of his professional life, and the example of his heart, which is attuned to the hurts of others. We have taught together for several years, and there has never been a single presentation where some idea of his has not influenced my thinking. I am grateful for his involvement in the concepts presented both in *Changes That Heal* and here in *Becoming an Adult*.

Dr. John Carter deserves many thanks for introducing me to the understanding of what an incarnational gospel really means, and to the understanding of the value of relationship at the center of any true scholarship. He was a model instructor at Rosemead Graduate School, and his continuing input over the years has shown me that Jesus holds all understanding in his hand.

Dr. Phil Sutherland's model of a wisdom perspective on the Scriptures gave me new lenses through which to view the Bible, and significantly helped me to discover "new wineskins" that could contain the true miracle of therapy. Everything that I think about the ways that humans grow contains the seeds of his perspective. I am thankful for his input into the early manuscript for *Changes That Heal* as well.

Dr. Bruce Narramore's thinking on the concepts of guilt and conscience, as well as on a process understanding of growth, were invaluable to me in my training. His commitment to training professionals has borne fruit for more than twenty years.

I will be forever grateful to Dr. Frank Minirth and Dr. Paul Meier, who encouraged me years ago to go into the field of helping. If it were not for them, I would certainly be doing something else with my life. And I am grateful to Dr. Althea Horner for her supervision and humanity. Her thinking about how people grow has been more than helpful to me as I have developed my own thinking. She has shown me that psychoanalysis must bow to love. Dr. Doug Wilson deserves special thanks for giving me a place to begin practice and for encouraging me to integrate that practice into ministry, as do the rest of CORE: Dr. Michele McCormick, Monte Pries, Ann Huffman.

Campus Crusade for Christ deserves special thanks for the development of *Changes That Heal*. It was under their original request that this material was developed and envisioned. Loren Lillestrand, then US field director, put the original project together, and deserves much credit for its coming to fruition. In addition, other Crusade staff members have been very encouraging in the development of this work. Special thanks go to Mary Graham for thinking that this could be used in training and Melanie Ahlquist for reading the manuscript.

The staff at the Minirth-Meier Clinic West have been superior models to work with. Their continued commitment to healing in the lives of others has encouraged me professionally as well as personally. I love seeing the fruits of their daily gifts to others. Dr. Dave Stoop was a constant encouragement in the writing of *Changes That Heal*, and his input as he taught the material with me was invaluable. Thanks goes to him for helping bring metaphor to life. Thanks also goes to the Friday group for their application of faith to life.

Also I'd like to thank Dr. Anita Sorenson for reading the *Changes That Heal* manuscript and making some helpful observations. I appreciate the support that Jana Swanson has offered personally and for interacting with the material.

Thanks to Scott Bolinder for believing in *Changes That Heal* and for agreeing to publish the revised edition, to Sandy Vander Zicht for her thoughtful and meticulous work in making the manuscript more user-friendly, to the rest of the Zondervan team for their encouragement and welcome, and to Sealy Yates for all of his encouragement and support and for the invaluable role he plays in the lives of Christian authors.

I am grateful to Maureen Price, Jody Coker, Lisa Leets, and the Growth Skills Foundation for their incredible work in getting this message to so many pastors and churches over the years. And many thanks to all the churches that have used *Changes That Heal* to help so many people.

If anything comes through in the message of these books, it is that the body of Christ is the only place in which we grow and become spiritually mature adults. My community of friends has been the place where I have "grown into" the concepts presented here. They deserve special thanks: Dr. Edward Atkinson for being a true friend through the years and showing me the Lord when he was not easily found; Bill and Julie Jemison for taking in a new Christian and walking through the early days of faith—their love and support

ACKNOWLEDGMENTS

will never be forgotten; Guy and Christi Owen for their supreme ability to produce a safe harbor for me; Toby Walker for keeping theology practical and being a truly giving friend; and my parents, whose early and sustained commitment to me have imparted much toward my ability to see God as good.

INTRODUCTION

The freedom associated with adulthood can be terrifying and misleading. At the ripe age of eighteen, you're officially legal and expected to make sense of all the social and legal concepts associated with becoming an adult. Adulting requires grownups to address time management, encounter financial barriers, embrace a growth mindset, make life-changing career decisions, identify balance amongst all things, and much more.

This book is a resource to help you navigate adulting. Compared to previous generations, young adults born in the 80s, 90s, and early 2000s have been slow to reach life milestones traditionally associated with adulthood, such as getting married, having children, living independently, and creating their own households. According to Pew Research, nearly one in three adults in the US shared a household.[1] Such living arrangements have caused the household formation rate for young adults to trend down in recent years.

There are several preconceptions tied to adulting—not to mention we have also lived through a pandemic and in the last twenty years have been introduced to life-changing technology. Even though there is no official manual to adulting, I am hopeful that this book will shift your perspectives and give you the knowledge necessary to be a happy and successful adult.

CHAPTER 1

WHAT IS ADULTHOOD?

Sara was anxious about everything. "I'm never able to relax," she admitted to me at her first counseling session, "no matter how well things are going or how successful I am. I always think something's going to go wrong, or that I haven't done quite enough."

She worried most about what other people thought of her. Constantly on her guard, she did everything she could to make sure her superiors approved of her work.

In addition, Sara always had an older woman in her life whom she looked up to but could somehow never please. From her early twenties till her late thirties, she was tormented by these women who were always proper, sweet, and concerned, but who had a critical streak in them a mile wide. "Your living room would look warmer if you changed the color of your drapes," they'd say. Or "If you were stricter in your discipline, your children would obey you more readily." Whatever their opinion, she would faithfully comply and await their approval. When they didn't approve, she would feel enormously guilty, but when they did approve, she could get only short-lived satisfaction.

Not only was Sara striving to please these women, but she also labored to please her husband. She sought his approval and felt horrible if she did not receive it. Sexually, she was uneasy and unfulfilled, always wondering if she had performed "well enough" and never feeling satisfied herself. Over the years she had steadily lost interest in sex, but she did not like her husband to see her as cold.

Poor Sara. What was she doing wrong?

Sara was one-down in all her important relationships. Her husband and these women were above her, and it was her task to gain their acceptance and approval in order to feel like she was okay. Like a child, she continually sought parental approval. She was a "little person in a big person's world."

Sara was not able to enjoy peer relationships with other adults. The freedom that adults have—to make their own decisions without permission from others, to evaluate and judge their own performance, to choose their own values and opinions, to disagree with others freely, and to enjoy sexual relations with an equal spouse—somehow had escaped her. Does Sara's adulthood sound similar to your own? You are not alone.

BECOMING SEPARATE

After a year of bonding and attachment, the process of separateness begins to "kick in" for an infant. They develop wonderful new abilities called secondary processes because they develop secondarily to the primary processes of feeling and loving.

Secondary processes promote separateness and identity; they are based in mobility, language development, development of thinking and language-based thought, realization of consequences and the law of cause and effect, more ranges of behavior, realization of increasing physical and emotional separateness, and the beginnings of the process of "willing." Since these sound like wonderful things, it's strange that some call this time the "terrible twos!" (I heard a friend of mine call this time the "terrific twos"; she relished her child's budding autonomy and separateness. It was a refreshing comment to hear.)

As these processes unfold, the entire world turns around for the child and the mother. What was formerly pretty much a unit becomes more of a relationship between two separate people. Think of the wonderful way in which God has designed the process: Trust and relationship is established in an initial bonding period, and from this trust comes the working out of a separateness that is not frightening because of the bond. It is the basis for what God calls bond servanthood in the New Testament. Because of our love for God, he can give us the freedom of our separateness. The relationship keeps us "in check." Love constrains us.

As love is established between an infant and mother, the child begins to slowly work out his sense of separateness from her. He is beginning to realize his boundaries and sense of separateness from mother. He is beginning to realize what is "me" and what is mother. As the infant gains the ability to move around, he begins to walk away from mother. He is learning to have a life of his own, albeit a small one. He is exploring the world "apart" from the one he was once "a part of." The budding faculties we mentioned above all aid in this process. As he gains mobility he can get farther away from his mother on his own. He can venture out, and all separateness for the first time is not caused by her. It is caused by his wishes to move away and explore by himself.

As his capacity for thought grows, he can better negotiate the world he is exploring and can even begin to name things. He begins to order his world. He realizes what things are and how to use them in a goal-oriented way. He can talk about them, ask for them, demand them, scream when he does not get them. He is learning how to think about and talk about a world apart from mother.

At the same time, he is learning increasing separateness from mother in other ways. He learns that when he walks, he sometimes falls down as a result of his actions, not hers. When he takes a tumble or discovers things, he feels the pain of falling or the joy of discovery; as mother shares these experiences with him, he learns to value and own them.

Similarly, he learns that he has certain abilities to do things. This is the beginning of competency and goal-directedness. Along with that, he learns that there are limitations on what he can do and that sometimes he needs help. An important aspect of boundaries is feeling both the elation and accomplishment of his separate behavior as well as its consequences. He needs to learn that there are limits to what will be allowed, and there are consequences to his omnipotence. He is gradually learning to "co-operate" with the world.

The child learns that he can want some things and get them, either by his own efforts or through someone's help, but he will not get everything he wants. Internal boundaries on desires are being created.

He realizes that he is responsible for his choices. If he chooses to hit his sister, for example, there are consequences. If he chooses to wander into the street, there are consequences. (This is a description of a process of gaining separateness, not of child discipline. Therefore, I will not go into specific consequences for behavior at various ages.) If he walks to the window, he experiences the good consequence of seeing a beautiful flower. He discovers the law of cause and effect: "My choices to be mobile can bring me pleasure." At the same time, choices can bring pain. "When I choose to touch the heater, it hurts."

Through every action, feeling, and choice, the child comes to an increasing realization that he, not his mother, is responsible for these things. He also learns that his thoughts and feelings are not always the same as his mother's. He may think it is a great idea to stay in the sandbox longer, but she thinks it is time for a nap. He may not wish to take a bath, but she wants him to. If he is allowed to have his thoughts and wishes without having all of them gratified, he learns how to own what he thinks, feels, and chooses, without being out of control. This is the delicate balance of being allowed to "be all of who he is" and not being able to be "all that there is." This is the balance of being able to have a self without being self-centered.

Failures in development of boundaries occur in both extremes. Some people's boundaries are confused because they are not allowed to own their feelings, thoughts, and behaviors, so they never own who they are. They don't know how to deal with these things later; they have no map. Other people, not limited enough in their feelings, thoughts, and behaviors, think they are the only ones who matter. These two later become the over-responsible and the under-responsible people.

Increasing Separateness

From the second year of life onward, bonding and separateness must work hand in hand. As children reach age four or five, they increase the separateness to include more and more people in their world. They learn to relate to two people at a time instead of only one. They have playmates and kindergarten friends as well as more and more experiences. Their world away from their primary attachments is growing, and they can stand to be away from them for more than twenty minutes. They can spend a whole half day at kindergarten and enjoy it instead of finding it overwhelming.

As abilities, thinking, behaviors, and feelings develop, separateness extends into the world of school. They have more and more responsibility as they own more things within their boundaries. Later, they move out of the house and go to college or get a job. Those who go to college eventually move from the safety of college into the "real world." All along, they learn how to stay in relationship, but increase in the ability to be a separate person from the ones that they are bonded to. This enables them to lead full, productive work lives and to be relational people. Love and work come together through the balancing of bonding and separateness.

WHEN WE FAIL TO DEVELOP BOUNDARIES

Ownership is crucial in creating boundaries. On the one hand, people who are not allowed to own their own thoughts, feelings, attitudes, behaviors, desires, and choices never develop a true sense of responsibility. They continue to have conflicts between bonding and separateness. They do not know how to have a relationship and at the same time be separate. They don't know that each person is responsible for each of the elements that are within their boundaries.

On the other hand, people who own other people's thoughts, feelings, attitudes, behaviors, desires, and choices extend their boundaries too far, encroaching on other people's property. This is what happened with Sandy and her mother. Sandy's time belongs to her; her mother's time belongs to her mother. However, Sandy had never learned to limit her mother.

Ownership is

CRUCIAL in CREATING

boundaries.

For years she allowed her mother to think that her mother owned her time as well. Sandy was not free to give time to her mother as she "purposed" in her heart; she was "obligated and compelled" to give to her mother what her mother felt she owned anyway: Sandy's life. The wish to control someone else's life and not allow their separateness is a serious relationship destroyer. It is a major source of more parent-child struggles, friendship struggles, marital breakups, work conflicts, and struggles with God than any other dynamic.

When the first human beings sinned and fell from grace, our boundaries were destroyed. Since we no longer had grace, we could not tell the truth about who owned what. Adam said it was the woman's fault, not his. She "caused" him to do it. Eve said it was the serpent's fault, not hers, for he "made her do it." They could not admit that their own desires, attitudes, and behaviors led to their choices. They could not take responsibility for themselves. They wanted to eat the fruit and to become godlike. They thought that they should have whatever they wanted, and that God really did not know what was good for them. They chose to reach past their allotted boundaries. And God held them responsible for all of those choices.

Since the fall, we have all had difficulty owning what is ours. We disown what is ours and try to own what belongs to others. Sandy's mother disowned her responsibility to raise a daughter who would grow up and leave her parents, clinging to others in adulthood. She disowned her responsibility for her disappointment in Sandy's not coming home for Thanksgiving. Just as the two-year-old has to deal with his disappointment of not being able to stay up all night with Mommy, Sandy's mother has to deal with her disappointment in not having Thanksgiving the way she wants it. Sandy's mother also tried to own things that were not hers, like Sandy's time and course of life.

Parents, children, friends, and spouses often have trouble working this out. There are two wills in any relationship, so allowances have to be made if love and responsibility are to be forthcoming. I saw a bumper sticker that read, "If you love something, set it free. If it really loves you, it will return. If it doesn't, *hunt it down and kill it!*" We all feel this way to varying degrees.

There are **two wills** in any RELATIONSHIP, so **allowances** have to be made if LOVE and RESPONSIBILITY are to be **forthcoming**.

We may want the people we love to be able to make their own choices, but many of those choices are going to limit us in some way. And when they do, we do not naturally want to deal with those limitations responsibly. We would rather blame.

CHAPTER 2

BOUNDARIES

Numerous problems arise when we fail to set good boundaries and maintain them. If we do not realize what we are responsible for and what we are *not* responsible for, we can suffer from the following symptoms. Symptoms, you recall, point to the existence of an underlying problem. Few people have ever come in to my office and said, "Dr. Cloud, I have trouble setting boundaries, and I need your help in learning how to set good boundaries." But people do seek help for the following symptoms, when their real problem is often confusion about where and how to set boundaries.

SYMPTOMS OF FAILURE TO SET BOUNDARIES

Depression

Many people experience depression because they do not set good boundaries. The lack of boundary setting sets them up for being mistreated, and much pain follows.

Others are depressed because they turn their anger inward at people who are controlling them. If they aren't in touch with their choices, they think they have no choices, that other people have control over their choices. They become resentful, perhaps even bitter.

Panic

Panic disorders—attacks of sudden, overpowering fright—most often fall in this category. Many people panic because they think they have no control over what happens to them. They think they must do whatever anyone wants them to do, and they feel out of control. Having others in control of one's life and choices can be very scary. It's a prescription for panic disorder.

Resentment

Many people resent certain things because they are doing them "reluctantly or under compulsion" (2 Corinthians 9:7). To comply with others' wishes, they do what they really don't want to do, then resent it later. Martyrs—people who assume an attitude of self-sacrifice or suffering in order to arouse feelings of pity or guilt in others—often display this symptom. Their giving is not really giving because it has strings attached.

Passive-Aggressive Behavior

Passive-aggressive behavior is characterized by indirect resistance to demands for adequate performance in social or work settings. For example, if a woman is pressured to serve on the school's cultural arts committee, she may say yes and then resist passively by forgetting appointments, procrastinating on projects, or misplacing important materials. She did not have the courage to set proper boundaries and just say no to the request to be on the committee.

When we do not set limits and let our "yes be yes and our no, no," we may set those limits passively. Many who struggle with uncompleted promises to others are really being passive-aggressive. They express the aggression of saying no in a passive way.

Codependency

Codependency is a learned pattern of attitudes, feelings, and behaviors in which people seriously neglect their own health and well-being for the wishes of others. Codependent people always put the other person first, often to their own detriment. They do not see who is responsible for what and often enable evil. These people are always confused about boundaries. In taking responsibility "for" others, they fail to act responsibly "to" them.

Identity Confusion

Identity comes from owning who we are and realizing all of our attributes. People who are not taking responsibility for what falls within their boundaries, and not being separate from others, are unable to tell what is them and what is someone else. We need to know who we are apart from others.

Difficulties with Being Alone

Some people have not established good enough boundaries so that they are able to have a self apart from others. They fear being alone, for they will not be with anyone; there is no one inside. They do not have the internal structure to contain the love they have for and from others. They always have to be with someone to survive.

These people have not failed to bond, but they have failed to develop an internal structure to hold the bonding inside. It is like pouring water into a cup with no bottom. The more love they get, the more they need. They have no ability to hold on to it. They need limits—boundaries—to help them form some internal structure.

Masochism

Masochists are people who get pleasure from suffering physical or psychological pain inflicted by others or by themselves. Masochists are unable to set limits on others' abusive behavior. They get a perverse pleasure out of being subjected to pain or humiliation. The pain causes more and more need, which makes it harder to set limits on the other person. They need someone so much, they can't limit them. Masochists need to establish a support network to learn to set limits on abuse.

Victim Mentality

People who suffer from a victim mentality see themselves as victims of circumstances and other people. They never take responsibility for themselves. They use words like, "I had to" and "I had no choice." Everything happens *to* them. They deny any sort of responsibility, especially in the areas of choices. They think they have no choices.

Blaming

Blaming is similar to victim thinking; blamers always direct responsibility for pain and change toward someone else. No doubt others cause us pain, but when we get into the "blame game," we make others responsible for dealing with our pain, and that keeps us stuck. People who stay in the blame stage never change, for they take no responsibility for making changes in their own attitudes, feelings, or behaviors, when such changes would ultimately help them.

Over-Responsibility and Guilt

People who do not have clear boundaries feel responsible for things that they should not feel responsible for, like others' feelings, disappointments, and actions. They feel guilty for not being what others want them to be and for not doing what others want them to do. They feel like they are bad for not carrying through on "their" responsibility: to make others happy.

Under-Responsibility

People who feel over-responsible for others often neglect their own backyard. They do not carry their own load (Galatians 6:5), for they are too busy carrying the load of others. In this typical codependent behavior, people feel so responsible for others that they do not deal with their own pain and life.

Feelings of Obligation

Paul mentions in 2 Corinthians 9:7 that people have these feelings when they are not choosing what they will give and what they will not give. They feel compelled to give to others; they are not free and in control of themselves.

Feelings of Being Let Down

Since many are so good at taking care of others, they feel that others are obligated to take care of them.

They feel let down when this doesn't happen. They perceive others to be unloving and uncaring if they aren't taking responsibility for them. They feel like they are the "givers" and others are "takers."

Isolation

People who experience boundary confusion, distorted thinking, and a lack of freedom often avoid relationship in order to feel a sense of boundaries. For them, getting close means losing their boundaries and ownership of themselves. It is so frightening and potentially conflictual that they eliminate relationship as an option and choose a world of isolation. Being alone means they won't be invaded or controlled.

Extreme Dependency

People who have never gotten a feeling of owning their own lives believe they can't function responsibly on their own. They will often depend upon someone else to negotiate the world for them, and they tend to fuse their identity with this negotiator. They are very fearful of separateness.

Disorganization and Lack of Direction

People who do not have a clear definition of themselves often lack direction and purpose. They cannot choose their own goals, likes, and dislikes. They get easily sidetracked by whatever anyone says to them, so they are scattered.

Substance Abuse and Eating Disorders

Many people who feel out of control of their lives turn to food, drugs, or alcohol to either dull their pain or to be able to take some control over something. This is especially true with people suffering from anorexia or bulimia. Boundaries are almost always an important issue in these disorders.

More often than not, boundaries are a strong issue in the resolution of addictions. Usually, when boundary conflicts are cleared up, when people with food or substance addictions begin to have a clearer sense of their own person, they begin to exercise self-control. Bulimics especially need to resolve issues of separateness. The ambivalence expressed in food is often resolved as the ambivalence of relationship is cleared up through boundary definition. They no longer express the "I want it, I don't want it" feeling by bingeing and purging.

Procrastination

Procrastination, or putting off unpleasant tasks until some future time, often results from a lack of clear boundaries. Procrastinators do not feel like they are really choosing; their no is not a real no. They say yes when they mean no; then they express their no through not following through. It is a distorted sense of control.

This is the dynamic that was operating in the parable of the two sons (Matthew 21:28–31). The procrastinating son was not honest about his no. Recall that he said yes to working in his father's vineyard, and then he never went. The other son first said no to his father, then changed his mind and went to work. This son could be honest about his no, so he could be honest about his yes also.

Impulsivity

Impulsive people invariably have a boundary problem. They lack internal structure. Whatever they think, they do; they have a limited ability to say no to themselves. As they clear up their boundaries and learn enough self-control to say "no," they begin to gain control of their impulses.

Generalized Anxiety

Some people struggle with a vague tension and anxiety that is sometimes related to lack of boundaries. Their internal lack of structure makes them unable to process and contain all the feelings they have, as well as to handle all the external demands. While these people often can't point toward one particular conflict or problem, they still feel anxious. Instead of working on a particular "issue," these people sometimes need to firm up their sense of who they are by creating stronger boundaries. This gives them a greater sense of self-control, a greater ability to process feelings, and, as a result, less anxiety.

Obsessive-Compulsive Behavior

Obsessive people are preoccupied with often unreasonable ideas or feelings; compulsive people have irresistible impulses to perform irrational acts. Obsessive-compulsive people struggle with both persistent preoccupations and irresistible impulses. For example, a man who feels compelled to wash his hands every hour would be displaying obsessive-compulsive behavior. This man is obsessed with the idea of catching a cold and feels compelled to wash his hands to prevent it.

Boundary setting is aggressive or bold behavior. People who can't set clear boundaries can turn this aggression against themselves in the form of painful obsessions or compulsions they must perform to be safe. People can often resolve these painful realities by strengthening their ability to set and keep boundaries. Setting boundaries helps provide the internal structure that can say no to both attacking thoughts and compulsions. They give them back the self-control that the compulsions were trying to provide.

By their very nature, compulsions indicate a lack of freedom. Developing boundaries and the ability to say no to others creates the freedom needed to work through compulsive problems.

SKILLS FOR SETTING BOUNDARIES

Let's look at some of the skills necessary for setting boundaries and learning to say no when someone tries to cross those boundaries.

Gain Awareness

Since setting boundaries is merely taking ownership of what is yours, your first step is gaining awareness of who you are. Become aware of your body, feelings, attitudes, behaviors, thoughts, abilities, choices, wants, and limits. Take inventory of where you have come from, where you are now, and where you are going.

Enlist others in taking inventory. You need feedback from others because you do not often see what you have disowned. You may even benefit from professional help. Proverbs 15:22 says, "Plans fail for lack of counsel, but with many advisers they succeed."

Define Who You Are

Just as God defines himself, you need to assert yourself. Begin to say what you feel, what you like,

Just as GOD defines **himself**, you need to ASSERT **yourself**.

what you want, what you will do, and what you think. Carve out an identity and say, "This is who I am."

Define Who You Are Not

You must also say who you are not. Say what is "not you," as well as what is you. Say what you don't agree with, don't like, won't do, and so on. People with boundary problems often do not stand against anything. They take everything in. This is very destructive. In Proverbs 6, God calls us to stand against and hate some things.

Develop the No Muscle

A child learns to set boundaries by saying "no." Many of us have eliminated this word from our vocabulary, and we need to rediscover it. Strengthen your no muscle. Begin with little exercises, such as saying no to dining at a certain restaurant that you don't want to go to, and work your way up to more demanding ones, such as saying no to lovemaking when it is not good for you. Learning to say no is probably the most important and difficult task in creating boundaries, especially saying no to parents when needed as an adult.

Stop Blaming Others

Taking responsibility for dealing with your own pain and not getting stuck in blaming others is a major move out of bondage and into health. Stop blaming others for your trouble, and deal with it. This does not mean that others did not cause it; it is fine to blame them for causing you pain. But to get out of it, you might have to take ownership of dealing with it and doing something about it. Staying stuck in blame is a dead-end street.

Stop Playing Victim

As an adult, you have choices. Begin to take responsibility for those choices and own them. If you are giving something, you are making a choice to give and you need to stop acting as if someone is making you give. As an adult, you are choosing. If you are working somewhere that you don't like, take responsibility for finding something else. If you are being criticized over and over by a friend, take responsibility to set up a meeting with him or her. You are responsible for what you choose to do. Taking this responsibility will change your life.

Persevere

God commands us to persevere, or to continue on in spite of difficulty or opposition. "Let us run with perseverance the race marked out for us, fixing our eyes on Jesus, the pioneer and perfecter of faith. For the joy set before him he endured the cross, scorning its shame, and sat down at the right hand of the throne of God. Consider him who endured such opposition from sinners, so that you will not grow weary and lose heart" (Hebrews 12:1–3).

Create goals for yourself and set about accomplishing them with continued, patient effort. Perseverance creates discipline and responsibility. Perseverance creates character. "Suffering produces perseverance; perseverance, character; and character, hope" (Romans 5:3–4).

Become Active, Not Reactive

People with boundary problems often see themselves not as initiators, but as reactors. They make choices by passively reacting to others. *Choose* to love and to give, don't just love and give when it is required. Choose to work and accomplish, don't just do it when it is required. This develops character. It develops a sense of "I will."

Set Limits

One of the most important tasks is setting limits on others' abusive behavior. Stop enabling others to be self-centered and irresponsible. Put limits on the ways that their substance abuse or physical abuse affects you. In addition, put limits on more subtle emotional abuse, such as criticism and blaming.

Begin to realize your limits of time, money, and energy. If you sow sparingly, you will reap sparingly; but if you sow more than you have, you will be bankrupt. Get with God and others to find what is reasonable for you at this time.

Choose Values

Define who you want to be and where you want to go. Choose for yourself this day whom you are going to serve. Decide what your values are going to be and work toward your goals. Other Christians may try to tell you what your values should be, but they are not perfect. You must take responsibility for your own choices.

Practice Self-Control

Set limits on your wishes. You can't have everything you want. Be careful not to go to the other extreme and put too many limits on your wishes, thereby controlling yourself out of having a "me." Strike a balance between satisfying your desires and controlling them.

Accept Others

Learn to love and accept others for who they are. If you don't, you are intruding on their boundaries and taking control of something that's not yours—their person. If you want to feel accepted, accept. If you want others to respect your "no," respect their "no." If you resent others for saying no to you, you will be confused about your own no and will be trying to control them. Love people when they say "no," and respect their freedom. Only then will you yourself be free.

Realize Your Separateness

Develop time and interests separate from the time and interests of those you love. Realize that separateness is good and will add to your relationship.

Time apart enhances the relationship by creating longing. Otherwise, you are clones. Counting the ways you are different from, as well as like, your loved ones will help your sense of identity.

Be Honest

Be honest with others. Many people will not be honest because they fear loss of intimacy and togetherness. In reality, honesty brings people closer together, for it will strengthen their identities. The more you realize your separate identities, the closer you can become. Telling loved ones what is really on your mind, and telling others what you really think, is the foundation of love.

Challenge Distorted Thinking

Jesus taught that truth sets us free. Identify your distortions and act in accordance with the truth; you will learn new ways of being and will produce a different kind of fruit. This is hard work and requires the help of friends and God's Spirit to lead you into the truth about yourself and about his world.

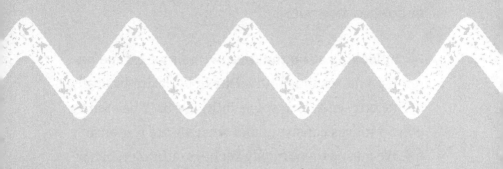

In LOOKING
at **boundaries**,
we cannot ESCAPE
one MAIN POINT:
responsibility.

In looking at boundaries, we cannot escape one main point: responsibility. Our boundaries basically define our sense of responsibility for us. They tell us what our lives consist of and what we are responsible for. We must own our body, feelings, attitudes, behaviors, thoughts, abilities, choices, desires, and limits.

If we were to stop there, behind carefully guarded fences, we would live a very safe but very unbiblical existence. This would fall short of love, the goal of life. The biblical concept of love involves loving and laying down our life for others. However, it is impossible to give away what we do not have, and boundaries are our way of "having" the self that we can then choose to give away.

Owning our own lives is the essence of freedom, and there is no love without freedom. Freedom realizes oneself, and love motivates us to give that self to others. When we give before we are free and truly own ourselves, we have fallen short of servanthood and into slavery. Realize what you own, and then share yourself with others. This is to fulfill the law of Christ.

CHAPTER 3

AUTHORITY AND POWER

Everyone who has ever lived has encountered a particular problem: being born a little person in a big person's world and being given the task of becoming a big person over time. We are all born children under adult authority, and over time we are to become authorities ourselves and be in charge of our lives.

This chapter will explore the problem of coming out from under a one-down relationship to the adult world and assuming one's role as an adult equal with other adults. *Becoming an adult is the process of moving out of a "one-up/one-down" relationship and into a peer relationship to other adults.* Becoming an adult is assuming the authority position of life, an important part of the image of God.

Authority has a number of different facets: power, expertise, office, influence, and submission. Adults have the *power* or right to give commands, enforce obedience, take action, or make final decisions. Adults often derive authority from their *expertise* or knowledge.

AUTHORITY

has a number of

DIFFERENT facets:

power, expertise,

office, **influence**,

and submission.

They also have authority because of their *office*, or the position they hold. Parents, for example, have authority over children because they are parents. In addition, adults have *influence* in the arena in which they operate. What they do affects other people. A final part of being an authority is to be able to give up rights and serve others in submission.

In terms of functioning in the image of God, we need to have command over our lives and the domain God has given us, officiate a role or office when asked, influence out of real ownership of something, have expertise, and submit to the authority of God and others without conflict. No wonder growing up is so hard to do. Many forces and circumstances interfere with the process; nevertheless, we must accomplish the task to function successfully as real image bearers. If we don't attain this position of adulthood, if we stay a child in our adult years, we will suffer significant psychological and emotional distress.

Adults who have not yet become "big people" feel one-down to their contemporaries, or they defensively take the position of being one-up on everyone else. In either case, the developmental task of establishing equality with other adults is imperative if guilt, anxiety, depression, sexual dysfunction, talent development, and spiritual bond servanthood are to be worked through. The developmental process is one of starting life from a position of one-down to the adult world, and gradually growing in stature and wisdom (Luke 2:52) to the point of being an adult in an adult's world.

Becoming an adult is a process of taking on more and more power and responsibility as we become old enough to handle them. Adults identify with the adult role enough to be able to do grown-up things without conflict, including developing a career, engaging in sexuality, establishing mutual friendships, treating other adults as peers, and having opinions. Adults establish a sense of competency over their lives.

This process of starting as little people and becoming equal with big people begins with bonding, having boundaries and separateness, and resolving good and bad, but ultimately has to do with *coming out from under the one-down relationship that a child has to parents and other adults and coming into an equal standing as an adult on his or her own.* This is the final step of development so that one can exercise the gifts and responsibilities God has given. It is a big leap into adulthood, but we are supposed to become equal with other adults. Then we can all be siblings—brothers and sisters—under the fatherhood of God.

Jesus calls us out of the one-down relationship to other people but encourages us to have respect for the role of authority at the same time:

> "The teachers of the law and the Pharisees sit in Moses' seat. So you must be careful to do everything they tell you. But do not do what they do, for they do not practice what they preach. They tie up heavy, cumbersome loads and put them on other people's shoulders, but they themselves are not willing to lift a finger to move them.
>
> "Everything they do is done for people to see: ... they love to be greeted with respect in the market-places and to be called 'Rabbi' by others.
>
> "But you are not to be called 'Rabbi,' for you have one Teacher, and you are all brothers. And do not call anyone on earth 'father,' for you have one Father, and he is in heaven. Nor are you to be called instructors, for you have one Instructor, the Messiah."
>
> —*Matthew 23:2–5, 7–10*

He says to do what Moses commanded, but not to consider other *people* as above us. Do not see them as fathers, for God is the father of Christian adults, and adults are all brothers and sisters. Do not see others as the ultimate leader, for Christ is the leader. He is calling us to the mutual equality of believers, but he is not doing away with the offices of authority others hold. We are to respect the offices of the church. We are to think of other people as equal siblings with us under God, even if they have an office. *To submit to them is to submit to God, not to people.*

People who believe others are above them are still relating from a child's position of being under a person, not under God. This belief makes the difference in one's ability to follow God and to seek God's approval instead of what people want. People who are stuck in this "people-pleasing" stage can't take charge of their lives as God commands. "Many even of the rulers believed in Him, but because of the Pharisees they were not confessing Him, for fear that they would be put out of the synagogue; for they *loved the approval of men rather than the approval of God*" (John 12:42–43 NASB, italics mine). These believers could not exercise their faith because they needed approval from human authority. They had not grown up.

Compare this to the statement about Jesus in Mark 12:14. "Teacher, we know that you are a man of integrity. You aren't swayed by others, because you pay no attention to who they are; but you teach the way of God in accordance with the truth." Jesus did not fear others; neither did he need their approval as parent figures. As a result, he could speak the truth to them and let them worry about whether or not they liked it.

In fact, Jesus implied that we are doing something wrong if everyone likes us: "Woe to you when everyone speaks well of you, for that is how their ancestors treated the false prophets" (Luke 6:26). There has to be some sort of people-pleasing going on when everyone speaks well of us! We have to be speaking from both sides of our mouth. People-pleasing can even keep one from seeing what is true from God: "How can you believe since you accept glory from one another but do not seek the glory that comes from the only God?" (John 5:44).

Paul also talked about getting out from under the "approval-of-people" trap: "We speak as those approved by God to be entrusted with the gospel. We are not trying to please people but God, who tests our hearts" (1 Thessalonians 2:4). Both Jesus and Paul realized that to do the authoritative work of adulthood, one could not be seeking the approval of other adults. That is what children do, and children cannot do adults' jobs! Therefore, seeking the approval of God and not trying to please others is an important aspect of growing into adulthood.

Adults make decisions, have opinions, establish values not subject to approval or disapproval from parents or parental figures, and incur legal consequences for their actions. Along with adulthood comes enormous freedom and responsibility, but the main theme is this: adults don't need "permission" from some other person to think, feel, or act. And adults are accountable for the consequences of the things they think, feel, and do.

Sara is a good example of someone who has not become an adult. She does not have the internal "permission" from herself, as the manager of her life, to do and think as she sees fit; she invariably needs approval and permission from some parental figure in her life. She will be burdened by enormous and unending anxiety until she is able to come out from under the pharisaical domination of others.

Becoming an adult is a process of gaining authority over our lives. You can probably think of people who have "taken charge" of their lives, who function as adults. They know what they believe, think through things for themselves, make decisions, do not depend on the approval of others for survival, and have an area or areas of real expertise. One gets a sense from being around these people that they are authoritative. They have become adults.

You probably also know people who seem wishy-washy, who look for other people to tell them what to think and believe, blindly following whatever the last "authority figure" has said. They are easily swayed by the thoughts and opinions of others. Others can make them change direction with a word. Others have too strong an influence over their identity, leaving them with strong feelings of guilt and anxiety. They have not become adults.

These are all issues of becoming one's own adult so that one can submit to the authority of God by choice. Let's look at the biblical basis for authority.

THE BIBLICAL BASIS FOR AUTHORITY

In the beginning, God made a glorious creation and entrusted it to human beings to govern and rule. He placed Adam and Eve in a position of authority over the creation:

> "Let us make mankind in our image, in our likeness, so that they may *rule* over the fish in the sea and the birds in the sky, over the livestock and all the wild animals, and over all the creatures that move along the ground." . . .
>
> God blessed them and said to them, "Be fruitful and increase in number; fill the earth and subdue it. Rule over the fish in the sea and the birds in the sky and over every living creature that moves on the ground."
>
> —Genesis 1:26, 28 *(italics mine)*

Inherent in this lofty position of authority was the power to determine the entire course of the creation. God gave humankind freedom to be a real authority

over creation, with real responsibility and real consequences. This was no dress rehearsal. "Now the Lord
God had formed out of the ground all the wild animals
and all the birds in the sky. He *brought them to the*
man to see what he would name them; and whatever
the man called each living creature, that was its name"
(Genesis 2:19, italics mine). Listen to the incredible
delegation of power and autonomy in this phrase,
"whatever the man called each living creature, that
was its name."

The one condition to this lofty position of authority
was submission to a higher authority: God. God told
Adam and Eve to do all that was delegated to them
freely, but they needed to stay within the parameters
God gave them. They were not to usurp the authority
of God by eating "from the tree of the knowledge of
good and evil" (Genesis 2:17). God warned them against
trying to function past their given authority. If they did
that, they would die.

This is the model. God grants us a lofty position of
rulership and authority, of adulthood and responsibility, of freedom to be "in charge" of our lives. Along with
this comes the responsibility of submitting to God's

authority and the accountability if we fail. Note three aspects of "being in charge": authority, responsibility, and accountability.

The enormity of this trust is evident in the nature of the fall. When Adam and Eve defied the authority of God, the consequences were grave. We all suffer for the movement the first couple made out from under the authority of God. We also feel the individual consequences when we fail to take authority over our own lives. In short, when we act like children with our adult responsibilities, we run into trouble. This is what Adam and Eve did. They listened to what a serpent said without even questioning, and with disastrous results.

Maybe you can feel the individual consequences of your failure to take authority over the domain God has given you to manage. Maybe your finances are a wreck, or you don't know what you believe about certain doctrines, or your children are out of control, or your talents are undeveloped. Whatever the area, when we do not take charge of whatever God has given us to do, we fall from the position God has given, with serious results. This is not punishment from God; it is a validation of the amount of trust and responsibility he has given us.

This is the authoritative position God first gave to us. But after the fall of Adam and Eve, we were no longer in a free position to take authority over life. Instead, we became slaves, with sin having authority over us. The entire book of Romans is dedicated to the theme of how we lost our freedom and became slaves to sin and how through grace we are returned to freedom and can now be servants of righteousness (Romans 6:17–18).

Redemption is a reversal of the effects of the fall—a return to the freedom and authority we had in the beginning. We are now in a position where we can be united with the "new Adam," who is Jesus, and it is impossible for him to rebel against God! This last Adam became "a life-giving spirit" (1 Corinthians 15:45). Therefore, to be united with Jesus is to be restored to a real position of authority that cannot fail. So great a salvation!

Our task of regaining our authority over life, then, is directly related to how much we walk "in him" (Colossians 3:3; 1 John 2:4–6; 1 John 1:5–7; Colossians 2:6).

He cannot fail in his task as the second Adam, and the more we identify with him, the more we become like him, the less we fail in taking authority over our lives.

Authority has existed from the beginning, with God being the ultimate authority over all. As God is an authority, we are to be authorities as his image bearers.

In the Old Testament, God placed many people in positions of authority over others. "Choose some wise, understanding and respected men from each of your tribes, and I will set them over you" (Deuteronomy 1:13). He always wanted his kings and leaders to walk with him, however, and to lead his people to him and his ways. There were lines of authority in the law and authority structures in individual families. The three principles present in the Garden of Eden remained: authority, responsibility, and accountability.

Parents, for example, were placed in authority over children, to teach them about God and to lead them in his ways. "These commandments that I give you today are to be on your hearts. Impress them on your children. Talk about them when you sit at home and when you walk along the road, when you lie down and when you get up" (Deuteronomy 6:6–7). Parents are God's representatives of authority in the child's life, so that the child can later be turned over to the direct father-hood of God and his authority.

As children gain this direction from their parents, they internalize these things into an obedient heart and are prepared to follow their heavenly Father in the same way as their earthly father. "Honor your father and your mother, as the LORD your God has commanded you, so that you may live long and that it may go well with you in the land the LORD your God is giving you" (Deuteronomy 5:16). As children are nur-tured and raised in the things of the Lord, they identify through obedience with the statutes and ways of God. In the Old Testament this ensured wisdom and good tribal relations that would allow them to do well for the rest of their lives. If they learned the right way to live and could get along with the extended relatives, they could have a smooth road ahead of them.

The role of authority in the Old Testament is an important aspect of the image of God. It started with God's delegating authority to Adam and Eve, then to Moses and the patriarchs, then to the different judges and kings, until the prophets began telling of the coming of Christ. At that time, the real King would come, the One to whom all authority is given. He would set up his own kingdom and have authority over it.

Then, as he established this authority, everything would be in subjection to him. From this position of authority, he would submit to the Father and *would reestablish God's ultimate authority.* Paul told us of this in 1 Corinthians 15:22–28:

> For as in Adam all die, so in Christ all will be made alive. But each in turn: Christ, the firstfruits; then, when he comes, those who belong to him. Then the end will come, when he hands over the kingdom to God the Father after he has destroyed all dominion, authority and power. For he must reign until he has put all his enemies under his feet. The last enemy to be destroyed is death. For he "has put everything under his feet." Now when it says that "everything" has been put under him, it is clear that this does not include God himself, who put everything under Christ. When he has done this, then the Son himself will be made subject to him who put everything under him, so that God may be all in all.

This is the plan of redemption. Christ would get back what God lost by taking authority; then he would give it back to God, submitting to his authority. His ability to be authoritative would enable him to recapture what was lost and give it back to God, who gave him the authority to do that. What an awesome plan!

The same thing God did with him, Jesus does with us. He gives us authority in him to take back what was lost, to reclaim it, then give it back to him, and he can give it back to the Father. In a real way, God is allowing us to take part in the war to regain what was lost. To do that we must do the two things Jesus did.

First, we must submit to authority and learn obedience. "In the days of His flesh, He offered up both prayers and supplications with loud crying and tears to the One able to save Him from death, and He was heard because of His piety. Although He was a Son, He learned obedience from the things which He suffered" (Hebrews 5:7–8 NASB). We must learn to obey first from parents, then from the Lord. This allows us to be perfected through discipline. "And having been made perfect, He became to all those who obey Him the source of eternal salvation" (Hebrews 5:9 NASB).

JESUS gives us **authority** in him to take back what was lost, to **reclaim** it, then give it back to him, and he can give it back to the **Father**.

We must be able to submit to the authority of God in Christ and to internalize his image.

Second, we must take authority over what is delegated to us and redeem what has been lost so we can give it back to him. We must take the role of authoritative ruler in the domains of our lives and follow his example in order to be agents of redemption. Then, we will reign forever with him as a joint heir.

In the New Testament, Jesus takes authority over situations and asks us to do the same. Let's look at a few aspects of authority that Jesus exercised so that we understand how much authority we have been commanded to take.

Power

The people were all so amazed that they asked each other, "What is this? A new teaching—and with authority! He even gives orders to impure spirits and they obey him."

—*Mark 1:27*

He replied, "You of little faith, why are you so afraid?" Then he got up and rebuked the winds and the waves, and it was completely calm. The men were amazed and asked, "What kind of man is this? Even the winds and the waves obey him!"

—*Matthew 8:26–27*

Jesus showed that he had power to do things. He proved his authority by exercising power over certain situations.

Expertise

When Jesus had finished saying these things, the crowds were amazed at his teaching, because he taught as one who had authority, and not as their teachers of the law.

—*Matthew 7:28–29*

Jesus had knowledge of God's Word and skill in interpreting it. His listeners sensed his authority.

Office

"For as the Father has life in himself, so he has granted the Son also to have life in himself. And he has given him authority to judge because he is the Son of Man."

—*John 5:26–27*

Delegated authority is authority that is given to someone. Jesus receives his authority from the Father.

Influence

After Jesus drove an impure spirit out of a man in the synagogue, "news about him spread quickly over the whole region of Galilee" (Mark 1:28).

Through the exercise of his gifts, Jesus gained influence with people. People who are respected for their skills, knowledge, and talents have earned influence and can use it for good.

Submission

Jesus called them together and said, "You know that the rulers of the Gentiles lord it over them, and their high officials exercise authority over them. Not so with you. Instead, whoever wants to become great among you must be your servant, and whoever wants to be first must be your slave—just as the Son of Man did not come to be served, but to serve, and to give his life as a ransom for many."

—*Matthew 20:25–28*

An important part of being an authority like Jesus is to be able to give up rights and serve others. He submitted to the cross and to his Father. We are to model Jesus' submission; it is an important aspect of authority resolution.

> In your relationships with one another, have the same mindset as Christ Jesus:
>
> Who, being in very nature God,
> did not consider equality with God something
> to be used to his own advantage;
> rather, he made himself nothing
> by taking the very nature of a servant,
> being made in human likeness.
> And being found in appearance as a man,
> he humbled himself
> by becoming obedient to death—
> even death on a cross!
>
> —*Philippians 2:5–8*

Just as Jesus became an authority in these different aspects, we are to grow up and become an authority in exercising power, holding the offices he has given us, developing expertise, using earned influence, and submitting to others. Jesus led the way. He was a person like us, just without all the mistakes (Hebrews 4:15). Therefore, he can be our model, who was tempted in all of the problems of growing up but made it nevertheless. He can help us become an authority over our lives.

CHAPTER 4

CREATING A DEVELOPMENTAL PERSPECTIVE

f becoming an adult is a task that requires power and expertise, it's easy to see why it is so difficult. When we are born, we have very little of either. All of the power and the expertise is in other people, and we are so very much smaller than they are.

As we continue to grow, however, and increase in wisdom and stature, we gain more ability and expertise to do things through the processes of internalization and identification. We internalize aspects of our parents and begin to identify with them as role models. Through this identification with authority figures, we learn to take in their roles and become like them. This path to adulthood lasts about eighteen years or so.

The Early Years

In the beginning stages, the main internalization is love. Learning that the big person who takes care of us is loving builds a bond that allows us to internalize aspects of them. If this goes well, parents put limits on us, and after some conflict, we eventually learn that limits really are a good thing.

Gradually, we develop more and more expertise, and our parents delegate more and more tasks to us, in respect for our budding abilities. If we do those well, then more and bigger ones are given, and we become more and more able to handle more and more responsibility. Expertise, delegation, power, and accountability are all increasing. First, the child is allowed to ride his bike down the street; later, at age sixteen he may be allowed to drive the car to a neighboring city. "Whoever can be trusted with very little can also be trusted with much" (Luke 16:10).

As they continue to develop, children begin to internalize some of the standards of their parents, and performance becomes very important. Parental approval is the only way out of guilt at this time, so children increasingly repress their rebellious and competitive feelings toward their parents, even though these feelings are increasing. The guilt of wanting to usurp parents being too strong to fight, the child identifies with the competition and becomes like them.

Between ages seven and twelve, mastery of tasks and work roles become very important. School-age children are increasingly industrious and into skill development; play is like a job, learning the ways of the world. Childhood chums are very important at this time also.

The Role of Parents

While their children are growing into adults, parents, or the parent in single parent scenarios, can help or harm their children's identification with authority in each of its aspects.

Power

The power a child needs later to live out his adult responsibilities comes from an early identification with authority. If the nature of a parent's power is gentle, warm, and loving as well as firm, the child will sense that personal power is a good thing. If a parent exercises power either passively or harshly, the child will get a mixed-up notion of power.

On the one hand, if a child's model is passive, she doesn't learn a sense of personal power, and this can be disastrous. Jesus has called us to be able to stand, but if a child has no picture of a "standing" adult, how can she learn? She feels as strong as the adult, and that's a weak view of power. (This power is the power inherent in the parent's personality, not the power attributed to the office of parent. In this interpretation of power, the child feels as if she is with a passive person, a domineering person, or a healthy person with a good sense of personal power.)

On the other hand, if a parent uses power harshly and cruelly, the child develops a hate relationship with power and can't internalize it without conflict. The New Testament gives us two clear passages on this dynamic:

> Children, obey your parents in the Lord, for this is right. "Honor your father and mother"—which is the first commandment with a promise—"so that it may go well with you and that you may enjoy long life on the earth." *Fathers, do not exasperate your children*; instead, bring them up in the training and instruction of the Lord.
>
> —*Ephesians 6:1–4 (italics mine)*

Children, obey your parents in everything, for this pleases the Lord. Fathers, do not embitter your children, or they will become discouraged.

—*Colossians 3:20–21*

These two passages give us a clear picture of the two roles of child and parent. Children are to obey, and parents are to not inspire wrath or discourage the children. Children can't identify with someone they hate. They need to develop power, expertise, and influence for adulthood, but if they hate the source of those things, they will have conflict. They will have a difficult time both developing their own authority and later submitting to God's.

Sean was twenty-eight when he came in for counseling. He had been fired from almost every job he had had.

"Why does this happen?" I asked him.

"Well, those guys always order me around like I'm a nobody. I can't stand to be talked to like that. So I decide, 'I'll show them,' and then I do."

"But it always costs you your job. Is it worth it?" I asked.

"Every time," he said, definitively. "I'll never bow down to them that way. Nobody will ever do that to me again."

"Do what?" I asked.

Sean began to shake with anger. As we talked further, he described years and years of angry abuse at the hand of his authoritarian father. Hating all authority figures with a passion, he had not been able to learn to submit to them or act authoritatively in his own life. He was still an angry little boy in a power struggle with his father.

After a considerable amount of hard work, Sean was able to work through his problem with authority. He first had to deal with his overwhelming anger toward his father, then find some older men as mentors. With God's help, he became an adult and took charge of his life.

Mike had the opposite reaction to an exasperating father. He had always passively succumbed to his father and had almost totally rejected his own sense of power. Whenever any male figure told him what to do, he would just fold his cards. His life drifted by until he was well into his thirties, and he was plagued by feelings of insecurity and confusion. He had truly lost heart.

He joined a therapy group in which he met some powerful, as well as supportive, men. For about a year he avoided conflict with the other men, but gradually he began to challenge them. He found out he was capable of fighting back without being crushed as he had been as a child.

He took them up on their challenges in sports and other activities and reached a place where competition was fun again. He wasn't as afraid of winning as he had been in the past. He had found men whose egos could stand it. This newfound self-confidence carried over into the work world, and he gradually tried new risks and jobs. Through the mentoring and his challenging of these other authority figures, he overcame his fear of male authority.

Mike's passive solution was as disastrous as Sean's aggressive one. Neither one had been able to get their adult authority roles in order because their fathers had disobeyed God's command. One had provoked his son to anger; the other had discouraged his son.

Expertise

In growing up, a child should have ample opportunity to learn more and more expertise, and the parents should support this process. In addition, parents are needed to be models of expertise for the child to get a picture of the value of work and industriousness. Children can identify with these positive role models and learn that "a desire accomplished is sweet to the soul." They need to look up to their parents in order to learn how to strive for excellence, to develop self-esteem, and to worship someone other than themselves.

A child develops expertise as his individual strengths and talents are recognized and built up by his parents. One young man who came to see me described how he would spend hours and hours practicing baseball, only to have his father walk by and say nothing. When he wanted to try a new project, his father would throw cold water on the idea. In early adulthood, when he needed to go out and take on the world, he suffered major depression at the thought. He was totally overwhelmed: he had no picture of an encouraging parent figure to cheer him on and believe in him. No parent had built up his expertise.

As a child develops ability, opportunity is needed to accompany it. A child needs to get a sense of being good at trying and learning. Parents should reward effort by getting their children the resources necessary to develop to the next level. For example, a boy learning to play baseball doesn't need the best baseball bat in the store, but it would help to have some sort of bat available when the child is ready. If someone has the opportunity to *learn that they can learn,* the rest of life is a cinch. They develop basic belief in their ability to tackle any task. This is becoming an adult.

Correction

As we have seen earlier, the relationship of the ideal to the real needs to be loving and accepting while prodding onward. Good parenting follows this guideline, as God does with us. A child who is treated harshly for failure becomes afraid of trying. Fear of failure often comes from an authority figure's harsh reprimand for a mistake.

God's attitude toward us as we learn things is quite different. Hebrews 5:14 says that we learn through practice, or "constant use"; therefore, God works with us as we are learning and gaining experience. Parents are needed to treat their children with understanding and patience as they practice new skills. If parents do this, their children will love trying new things.

The book of Hebrews describes an authority who is very loving toward the process of growing up:

> For we do not have a high priest who is unable to empathize with our weaknesses, but we have one who has been tempted in every way, just as we are—yet he did not sin. Let us then approach God's throne of grace with confidence, so that we may receive mercy and find grace to help us in our time of need. Every high priest is selected from among the people and is appointed to represent the people in matters related to God, to offer gifts and sacrifices for sins. He is able to deal gently with those who are ignorant and are going astray, since he himself is subject to weakness.
>
> —*Hebrews 4:15–5:2*

Our High Priest (Jesus) corrects gently, for he empathizes with our weakness. If parents follow his lead, learning will be a joyful experience.

The Power of the Office

An office is a position of authority or trust. Because they hold the *office* of parent, parents have authority to enforce consequences. They are role models for their children as those children try to identify with authority.

In the story of Adam and Eve, God held an office as their authority. In addition, he gave them the office of steward. When their behavior was out of line, he showed the power of his office to enforce the consequences of their behavior. This instilled a basic view of the authority of God in the universe for eons to come. Human beings and the heavenly hosts learned that when God said something, he meant it.

Children who are raised in situations where authority has no power learn neither to respect authority nor to identify with it. According to researchers, models with these characteristics are more likely emulated: they are warm and loving; they possess some similarity to the person following them; they're not perfect but are coping with life; and they have perceived power.

Children who are RAISED in situations where AUTHORITY has no power **learn** neither to RESPECT authority nor to **identify** with it.

Thus, children in the developmental process need parent figures who are authoritative and who possess the power of their *office of parent*. The respect gained enables the child to follow the parents out of a healthy "fear"—a respect based in love. Loving power is the best power to identify with, and some of this power has to come not only from the personality of the parent but from his or her office of parent. Developing respect for this office lays a basis for the child's later respecting of the law, governing authorities, and church authorities (Romans 13:1).

This will also give them the ability to execute with authority whatever role they later play, whether it be homemaker, church leader, factory worker, or company president. They have a model in their head of what it means to take a role or office and execute it with authority.

Adolescence

If all of these processes go well, the stage is set for a healthy twelve-year-old to appear to "go crazy." Adolescence is the beginning of the undoing of the yoke of slavery called childhood. It is the beginning of stepping into an equal role with the adult world, and like every other overthrow of government, it usually doesn't occur without a rebellion.

The Bible compares childhood to slavery because a child does not yet legally own his or her own life.

> What I am saying is that as long as an heir is under-age, he is no different from a slave, although he owns the whole estate. The heir is subject to guardians and trustees until the time set by his father. So also, when we were underage, we were in slavery under the elemental spiritual forces of the world. But when the set time had fully come, God sent his Son, born of a woman, born under the law, to redeem those under the law, that we might receive adoption to sonship.
>
> —*Galatians 4:1–5*

From this slavery, children push back until they recognize their freedom as adults and can reidentify with this role. And that, my friends, can be a stormy process. During adolescence a little person is becoming a big person and trying to take the power over her life but is not quite there. The child, or near-adult, has one foot in each camp, and she is in the process of over-throwing authority and becoming her own person.

Adolescence is the time of questioning authorities and choosing things for oneself. In a real sense, parental *control* is gradually morphing in favor of parental *influence*. If parents have built up a good relationship with their child over the years, they can try to exert their influence over the child during this time period. But they will have little control. By this time, the child is big enough and mobile enough to do pretty much what he or she wants to do. They must enforce limits and consequences, but it is very difficult to control another adult. They can control only themselves and how they respond, giving the needed limits and con-sequences to someone they can no longer control, as many parents discover in power struggles.

In this wonderful time of life, all sorts of things prepare one for adulthood proper. The adolescent experiences power that is different from earlier times. He has real mobility and can often get work that pays more than babysitting. He has buying power, as well as intellectual power to begin to figure out the world and deal with it. The often-heard cry is, "Let me do it.

You always treat me like a child!" The adolescent is testing his own power to run his life.

Also, a shift in office occurs. Parents often lose some of the undying respect they once had at this time, and the adolescent listens to other authority figures outside the home. She learns that Mom and Dad are not the only ones who know anything. Youth leaders, teachers, and coaches become valuable sources of influence; their influence is even greater if they differ from parents! Heeding others' advice gives the child a feeling of independence from parents, which is the chief task of adolescence.

In addition, the peer group becomes the main attachment. As adolescents move into adulthood, they need the support of community and friends in addition to that of their parents. This move is healthy. By establishing strong peer relationships, they will have the ability to create support networks for the rest of their lives. Many people in their early thirties have never emotionally left home. When they try to separate from parents, they don't have the skills to build real support networks, and their move to adulthood doesn't work. They are stuck as children because they cannot depend on friends instead of parents.

Adolescents begin to recognize their real skills and talents so that they can take authority in this area. They pursue many activities and get the idea whether or not they like sports, academia, social concerns, or the arts. They aren't ready to pick a career, but they are discovering their basic interests and talents. They often run into problems with parents, for their interests may not be what the parents want for them. Parents need to negotiate this battle carefully, or they will lose worse in the end. Children begin to make choices, and their choices are to be respected. If they are truly destructive, limits are needed, but preserve their ability to choose. Bad choices should cost them so they can learn to use their control in healthier ways.

As they realize the abilities God has given them, they pursue things outside of home to nurture those talents. Sports teams, school clubs, service organizations, church groups, and explorer groups are invaluable for the teen to learn more about the world. Work should become more important, and teens should earn money in some substantial way. They also need to have the freedom to decide how they will spend it. If parents remember that adolescence is a boot camp for adulthood, they begin to ask this question, "What will help them prepare for when they will not be living here and have me around?" This takes much of the power struggle out of parent-adolescent relationships.

The teen years are a wonderful time of learning about the opposite sex and how to relate more intimately. They discover their bodies and feel things they have never felt before. They learn to relate in a deeper way, risking romantic attachment in a way that is much deeper than puppy love. They throw off the repression of the last decade of their lives, and they become a factory of impulses they have difficulty controlling. They also have difficulty understanding why they need to control them and need help.

They need sound guidance from parents and other authority figures that upholds the value of sex and gives proper guidelines and limits without being repressive. Most parents find this difficult because they fear their teen's sexuality. On the one hand, they do not want to destroy their view of sex; on the other hand, they want to set appropriate limits.

If PARENTS remember that **adolescence** is a boot camp for ADULTHOOD, they begin to ask this QUESTION, "What will **help them prepare** for when they will not be LIVING here and have me around?"

Teens also struggle with values. For the first time they are in a position to question what their parents have taught them to be true. They need to question the things Mom and Dad believe and come up with their own reasons for faith and other values. If their faith does not become their own, they will lose it later, or become Pharisees. Exposure to good youth groups and leaders is so important, for it allows opportunity to take doubts and questions to someone other than parents. Their friends will be giving them answers as well, so it is good to have solid youth leaders and peers to relate to and go through the "valley of the shadow of death of the childhood faith" with. The Bible provides many examples of people who have gone through this questioning period, including the prodigal son and the two sons in the vineyard.

Teens overthrow parental standards and select their own standards and values for life. Don't get me wrong; parents are significant in this process, but teens need freedom to think and choose, to question and doubt, especially later in adolescence and in early adulthood. In these times, other adults are very important in their lives.

If this process goes well, the people who come out the other end can be called adults. They are their own person, responsible for themselves, leaving home and establishing a life of their own with their own talents, direction, purpose, power, office, influence, and expertise. This is the process of becoming an adult, and one can see why it is not an easy one.

By this time, however, they need to have a good beginning in personal power, expertise, influence, office, and healthy submission. It's not complete at this time, just started down the right road. If good seeds are planted, as well as good experiences, they are prepared to dive into adulthood with all of its trials and victories. By this time, they have begun to think for themselves, stand on their own two feet, disagree with authority figures, and stand with their own opinions. They have the tools to be released from parents to the authority of God and the brotherhood of humankind.

The main issue here is that they feel adequate enough in those areas to come out from under the one-down position to adults they have had all their life. They feel more of an eye-to-eye equality to other adults and *are no longer looking to other adults to perform parental functions for them.* If they have reached adulthood, they do not look up to other adults for parental functions, such as thinking for them or telling them how to live and what to believe. Other adults are looked to as experts who can give advice and input, but each person is responsible for his or her own life. This is adulthood.

CHAPTER 5

THE SPIRITUAL IMPLICATIONS OF THE ADOLESCENT PASSAGE

t is essential to make the connection between this step of maturity and its spiritual implications. The adolescent passage is when we overthrow the legalistic structures that interfere with our relationship with God. We need to chisel away at the authority of our parents as godlike figures so that God can be our parent. In short, we need to put aside our parents so that we can be *adopted* by God. If we have never gone through that process, we will suffer from spiritual childhood and not be able to get out from under the law and the slavery of rules.

Paul equates these parental structures with the law, as we saw above. Looking again at Galatians 4:1–7 will help us to understand many spiritual problems people have.

Paul compares childhood to slavery (Galatians 4:3) and talks about children being "in slavery *under the elemental spiritual forces of the world*" (emphasis mine). These forces, referred to elsewhere as the rules of religion, are worthless in creating real maturity:

> Since you died with Christ to the elemental spiritual forces of this world, why, as though you still belonged to the world, do you submit to its rules: "Do not handle! Do not taste! Do not touch!"? These rules, which have to do with things that are all destined to perish with use, are based on merely human commands and teachings. Such regulations indeed have an appearance of wisdom, with their self-imposed worship, their false humility and their harsh treatment of the body, but they lack any value in restraining sensual indulgence.
>
> —*Colossians 2:20–23*

Basically, Paul says that we are to be freed from man-made rules and adopted as sons and daughters of God. This freedom from parental structures leads us to a love relationship with God and an obedience to his principles of love. It moves us from a rule-based way of thinking to a love-based way of thinking and enables us to work according to *principles* instead of rules.

However, if we have never questioned the authority of our earthly parents, the givers of the first law, we can't question the authority of the law itself and reject its ability to save us. This is why authority-bound people like the Pharisees are always so legalistic. They are always trying to be "good enough" to be accepted by their legalistic consciences. Listen to Paul's words:

> Before the coming of this faith, we were *held in custody* under the law, locked up until the faith that was to come would be revealed. So the law was our guardian until Christ came that we might be justified by faith. Now that this faith has come, we are *no longer under a guardian.*
>
> —*Galatians 3:23–25 (italics mine)*

We have to come out from under the law, for its guardianship is over. We are to be adopted by our new parent, God himself! Like Paul, we must reject the notion that, by obeying parental structures, we can save ourselves: "no one will be declared righteous in God's sight by the works of the law" (Romans 3:20). This puts us into a direct relationship to God as parent

We have to move past
the SYSTEM of RULES
and parental **governing**
of behavior to reach
a place of **freedom**
and OBEDIENCE
to the SPIRIT.

and out of the slavery of the legal mentality: "So you are no longer a slave, but God's child; and since you are his child, God has made you also an heir" (Galatians 4:7). This is a calling to the freedom of bond servant-hood with God, as opposed to a childhood system of rules. We have to move past the system of rules and parental governing of behavior to reach a place of free-dom and obedience to the Spirit.

Paul speaks of the nature of this freedom: "You, my brothers and sisters, were called to be free. But do not use your freedom to indulge the flesh; rather, serve one another humbly in love. For the entire law is fulfilled in keeping this one command: 'Love your neighbor as yourself'" (Galatians 5:13–14). He echoes Jesus' state-ments to the Pharisees, the authority-bound people of his time. Jesus called them to get out from under their parental-based rules and elementary ways of seeing and move toward love. They apparently had never gone through the adolescent questioning of their elders and fathers and come up with their own beliefs:

The Pharisees and some of the teachers of the law who had come from Jerusalem gathered around Jesus and saw some of his disciples eating food with hands that were defiled, that is, unwashed. (The Pharisees and all the Jews do not eat unless they give their hands a ceremonial washing, holding to the *tradition of the elders*. When they come from the marketplace they do not eat unless they wash. And they observe many other traditions, such as the washing of cups, pitchers and kettles.)

So the Pharisees and teachers of the law asked Jesus, "Why don't your disciples live according to the tradition of the elders instead of eating their food with defiled hands?"

He replied, "Isaiah was right when he prophesied about you hypocrites; as it is written:

"'These people honor me with their lips,
    but their hearts are far from me.
They worship me in vain;
    their teachings are merely human rules.'

"You have let go of the commands of God and are holding on to human traditions."

—*Mark 7:1–8*

The Pharisees' questioning of Jesus and judgment of his disciples came from their fusion with their parental figures and parental structures, "the tradition of the elders." They were not free enough from them to see the truth.

Jesus also accused the Pharisees of thinking it was more important to please parent figures than to please God. Again, another fusion with the ways of their fathers:

> "Woe to you, because you build tombs for the prophets, and it was your ancestors who killed them. So you testify that you approve of what your ancestors did; they killed the prophets, and you build their tombs."
>
> —*Luke 11:47–48*

Here Jesus says that to approve the evil deeds of our parents and parent figures is to become like them. He calls us to question our fusion with authority, leave that allegiance, and give our allegiance to Jesus (Matthew 10:34–37). Allegiance to him must be stronger than our earthly parent-child relationship, for our parental relationship must be to God.

How Jesus dealt with his parents when he began to assert his independence and purpose is also very instructive. Up until a certain age, Jesus was under his parents' authority, as was commanded in the law. But, in adulthood, things began to change. When Jesus was twelve, his parents noticed that he had separated from them to go to the temple. When they told him that they had been worried about him, Jesus answered, "Why were you searching for me? Didn't you know I had to be in my Father's house?" (Luke 2:49).

Another time he made it clear that he needed to obey God, not his mother: "Woman, why do you involve me? My hour has not yet come" (John 2:4). Jesus was growing up and transferring his parental allegiance to God, just as we all must do.

In all these examples, Jesus makes two points. First, we need to come out from under our parents' authority and give our allegiance to God. Second, when this happens, we need to shift our thinking from rules to principles.

Remember when the Pharisees criticized Jesus' disciples for picking grain on the Sabbath? He answered them:

"Haven't you read what David did when he and his companions were hungry? He entered the house of God, and he and his companions ate the consecrated bread—which was not lawful for them to do, but only for the priests. Or haven't you read in the Law that the priests on Sabbath duty in the temple desecrate the Sabbath and yet are innocent? I tell you that something greater than the temple is here. If you had known what these words mean, 'I desire mercy, not sacrifice,' you would not have condemned the innocent. *For the Son of Man is Lord of the Sabbath."*
—*Matthew 12:3–8 (italics mine)*

When Jesus says that the Son of Man is Lord of the Sabbath, he places himself above the rules. The rules were made to serve his agenda, and that agenda is love. Thinking has shifted from being rule-based black-and-white thinking to principle-based thinking that must be interpreted in light of love. Our obedience to Jesus must supersede our obedience to traditions of our parental figures.

Rigid, pharisaical people can't tolerate this teaching. If they don't have a strict rule to handle every situation, they are lost, and they will invent one, as the Pharisees did. The Bible tells us to love, and if we have to upset a "tradition of the elders" to love, so be it. The Pharisees' theology wasn't big enough to allow for the need of the person, be it hunger or healing (Matthew 12:10–12). Anytime someone's theology will not allow them to help someone who is hurting, their theology is not big enough to hold the love of God. They "condemned the innocent" (v. 7).

A spiritual leader once told me that if the only way an autistic child could be helped was through the intervention of therapy, it must be God's will for this child to suffer! He said he could not see therapy condoned in the Scriptures, and if this were what the child needed, it must be God's will for the child to stay cut off from love and relationship! His theology was not big enough for love to fit in. He was not free to "heal on the Sabbath" and he was condemning the innocent.

When people separate from these legalistic "elemental spiritual forces of this world," changes take place both in their reasoning and in their ability to love. Their thinking changes from rigid and concrete to principle based and symbolic. They begin to understand the mysteries of God and relate to him in love, applying his truth in wisdom and love, instead of hiding behind strict, legalistic formulas. The gospel becomes more of a relationship between God and people than a system of rules designed to keep people in control.

The ways people think about situations change, and they reason in the light of love. Paul, in the great love chapter, says the following: "When I was a child, I talked like a child, *I thought like a child, I reasoned like a child.* When I became a man, I put the ways of childhood behind me. For now we see only a reflection as in a mirror; then we shall see face to face. Now I know in part; then I shall know fully, even as I am fully known. And now these three remain: faith, hope and love. But the greatest of these is love" (1 Corinthians 13:11–13, italics mine).

When people begin to reason as adults, and not as black-and-white-thinking children, mystery and ambiguity become more acceptable, and love becomes most important. People who have not gone through the adolescent passage of coming out from under parental rules do not think they are seeing "only a reflection" or "in part." They think they have the "absolute" answer for everything.

When we become spiritual adolescents, we find ourselves clinging much more closely to God, our Father, for we need his direction through the fog. We are not so sure of everything, and our theology does not have an answer for every situation. We find ourselves needing a relationship with him, not just a system of rules. We go through our own Gethsemane, trying to submit to the will of God in the midst of the pain (Luke 22:42). There is no simple theological answer to pain; the answer is a relationship with God in the midst of pain. Those who need things in neat little black-and-white packages cannot tolerate such a faith.

People who make this transition let go of rules and get to a real, adoptive relationship with God the Father. Their reasoning changes to principle thinking instead of black-and-white rule thinking. Their theology changes from being based on the law to being based on love, and their faith changes from an ethical system to a relationship with God. Rejecting the "traditions" of people and looking inside to find the real, impulsive adolescent self that at times resembles utter chaos is the only way to a real relationship of needing a Father.

When PEOPLE begin to **reason** as adults, and not as black-and-white-thinking children, **mystery** and **ambiguity** become more acceptable, and **love** becomes most **important**.

When we let go of rules that "keep things in check," we find ourselves "poor in spirit" (Matthew 5:3) and in need of a Father. This is what being adopted is all about. This is redemption and spiritual adolescence. We must become aware of the rebellion underneath outward compliance, confess it, and be welcomed home by the gracious Father. That is faith that saves.

Coming out from under the parental bondage allowed spiritual greats, such as John the Baptist, to accomplish their work. John the Baptist stood against the parent figures of the day, calling them a "brood of vipers" (Matthew 3:7). Martin Luther stood up against the religious authorities of his time, who said that we could not have a direct relationship with God without intermediary interpretation.

It takes someone who feels equal to other adults to be able to do the things God asks us to do. We must own our lives and not need parental approval so that we "are not trying to please people but God, who tests our hearts" (1 Thessalonians 2:4). The next chapter shows what happens when we don't.

CHAPTER 6

WHEN WE FAIL TO GROW

My friend had one of those looks on her face that people sometimes have when they discover the truly profound. This was no exception. She said something I'll never forget: "You know something? Life is upside down."

"What do you mean?" I asked.

"We should be adults first, and then children. It's too hard the other way around."

Human development is complicated. When your childhood comforts and support are taken away, the transition of total independence can feel daunting and overwhelming.

SYMPTOMS OF AN INABILITY TO BECOME AN ADULT

Everyone who has ever lived (except Adam and Eve) has encountered the problem of being born a little person in a big person's world and being given the task of becoming a big person over time. We are all born children under adult authority, and over time we are expected to become adults ourselves and to take charge of our lives. This task, as my friend observed, is not easy. Some of us never accomplish it. We try to live adulthood from the one-down child position. Following are signs of this inability to achieve adulthood.

Inordinate Need for Approval

People who struggle with taking charge of their lives often cannot function independently of the approval of others. They strive constantly to gain the approval of some "significant other," whether it be their boss, their spouse, their friend, their pastor, or their coworker.

This kind of approval is different than the normal affirmation we all need for our work. We all need praise for a job well done. Approval becomes problematic when people don't feel good about themselves or the work until someone tells them that the work is good. They wait until an "authority" figure pronounces it good before they know that it is (and they are) good.

If the authority figure pronounces it good, their entire self-image changes. The other's opinion carries far too much weight and has taken on the role of judge and jury, or parent, for the person.

Fear of Disapproval

Fear of disapproval goes along with the need for approval. Often people are inordinately anxious whenever an authority figure is around. Their anxiety interferes with their ability to do the job well. Every time their work is to be evaluated, their fear is activated, or they have a constant fear of being evaluated.

One young graduate student would begin to have panic attacks near the end of every semester. Everything would be going well until three weeks before semester's end. At that time, he would go into a state of tension that would increase to panic. He would lose sight of the tasks at hand and begin to focus on whether or not his professors would like his papers.

His history revealed a perfectionistic father who would criticize his work harshly. Fearing his father, he had remained a submissive little boy well into his twenties. Because he had never come out from under his father's rule, adult authority figures still had the role of judge in his life. They had the power to render him a valid person or not, and exam time gave a platform for this dynamic.

Gradually, as he began to challenge the professors, he learned they weren't so powerful after all, and he eventually began to feel as if he were their equal. He got to where he could enter an exam without excessive anxiety. He had gone through a "rite of passage" of becoming equal with his father figures. He was a peer and no longer feared being judged.

Guilt

Guilt always has as a component the loss of parental approval. Therefore, often when one struggles with guilt, one still feels "under" the parental voice. The internal parent has not been dethroned so that it can't punish.

Guilt keeps the focus off the consequences. An adult conscience lives life according to real consequences, not guilt. If adults get a traffic ticket, for example, they feel bad about the money for the fine and may be sad because they violated a value. People in the child position feel more guilt than consequences.

GUILT keeps the **focus** off the consequences. An adult CONSCIENCE lives life according to **real consequences**, not GUILT.

People who have not grown up also feel pressured by credit card balances, bills, deadlines, assignments, and tasks. The demand itself is perceived like a parent; they feel pressure to comply or they are "bad." This comply-resist dynamic often ends up in a guilt-procrastination battle that makes them spend more.

Sexual Struggles

People who feel one-down to authority more often than not have sexual difficulty. The reason is simple: they have not gone through the adolescent passage of disagreeing with their parents and therefore overcoming guilt and repression. Sexuality is still a "no-no" to them because psychologically they are children who "shouldn't think about such things." Since children don't have sex, their thinking interferes with their sexual functioning. They can suffer from inhibition (which is usually fear of parental criticism), lack of orgasm, guilt, loss of desire, or performance anxiety.

When people feel like adults with other adults, their bodies are their own to give away to their spouses and enjoy as they please. Only then can there be mutual giving and receiving.

When Amanda got married, she suffered a complete loss of sexual desire. Sexuality had intrigued her before marriage, but after the wedding, the desire disappeared. After months of trying to regain the desire, she came into therapy.

As she began to unravel the problem, it became clear that she was still "Daddy's little girl." Her father was overinvolved in her marriage, and she was still experiencing a strong desire to please him as best she could. In a real sense, she had not left home.

Since she had not come out from under his authority, she was still a child inside, and children do not have sex. Since her main attachment was still to her father, not her husband, any sexual wishes were too incestuous or prohibited to handle. Consequently, she repressed her entire sexuality.

She worked hard to let go of her relationship with her father and her wish to please him. She even wrote him a letter, resigning from the job of making him happy. As she worked through this process, she moved from being a repressed little girl to being a sexual woman. Because she let go of her parent, her adolescent function of sexuality was able to emerge.

She began to enjoy sex very much and was more and more uninhibited. Her husband was happy about this result!

Fear of Failure

People still under their parents' domain fear failure because they fear the disapproval of their rule-bound conscience (Galatians 4:3; Colossians 2:20). They internally feel that their actions will be judged and disapproved. In biblical terms, they are still "under a guardian" (Galatians 3:25).

When they realize that they stand in grace "in Christ," the dynamic of being "under" a judge and waiting for a stamp of approval is changed (Galatians 5:1). They are free to practice without fear of failure and to learn without guilt and anxiety.

Need for Permission

Many struggle with an inordinate need for permission. They invariably think they need to get clearance from someone before they can proceed. They often ask, "May I say something?" in the middle of a conversation, when it's unnecessary to ask permission to speak. They are speaking from an internal state of bondage to a parental authority.

They hesitate to test the limits of any system or organization to find out what is okay and what isn't. Their bosses are often bothered by how much supervision and direction they need to make decisions because of their fear of "getting into trouble." It's as though they live in the small basement room of a large mansion. They are afraid to venture out and discover how big their living space really is.

"You Can't Do That" Syndrome

Authority-bound people tend to stifle creativity. Someone may come up with a new way of doing something, and the authority-bound person will say, "You can't do that," or "It'll never work." They appear to have prison bars around anything creative or new. They are pessimistic about trying new things, preferring the "tried and true." Or more accurately, "the tried and accepted."

They overidentify with their limiting and punitive parent, always giving restrictions and rules. They haven't thrown off their parents' restrictions and found their own. They are like robots who do whatever their parents say, even at age forty.

Inventors and entrepreneurs have no patience for people with authority problems and call them "tunnel-visioned" or "myopic." Everyone who has ever started a new business has heard discouraging messages from scared observers.

Feelings of Inferiority

The word *inferior* comes from a word that means "low" or "below." It is easy to see, then, how people who have been put down or held down by authority figures feel inferior. Often their parents have not treated them with respect as people in their own right, so they invariably look up to others and feel lower than them. They tend to think that someone else is always better in some way or always a model for them. They never feel equal.

Aaron's life was marked by feelings of inferiority. He felt one-down to most people he had contact with. A successful businessman, he had done well when he was in the servant position in business transactions as a subcontractor to the "big cheese contractor."

He worked hard at pleasing the person he was working for, and as a result, was rewarded.

At the same time, however, he suffered panic attacks when he had to work directly with contractors. He vacillated between fearing their disapproval of his ideas and being terrified that they would think he was too smart and resent him. He was in a bind that made his work life a wreck.

Competitiveness

Since getting to an equal stance with others means competing with our parents for the role of "boss," people who have never established equality with their parents act out unresolved competitive issues, often with people of the same sex.

Our earliest form of competition comes from same-sex parents. If we do not resolve this competition by identifying with our same-sex parent, lingering competitive struggles can follow us for a long time.

Competitive people are always trying to usurp the position of the "one-up" person. They cannot stand for anyone to win "over" them, for it puts them in a one-down position in their head. Instead of saying, "I lost the game," they say, "I am an inferior person." Therefore, they *must* win in order to not be inferior to anyone. They are often still trying to feel equal to Mom or Dad, so they see every situation competitively.

Loss of Power

Those who have not become an adult either repeatedly give away power in relationships or feel that they are losing power. On the one hand, these people do not see a good relationship as one in which two people mutually submit to one another's preferences in love; instead, they give all power to the other person and then obey this person like a parent. Being "in charge" is like a hot potato that needs to be passed along as quickly as possible.

On the other hand, these people lose power to controlling and domineering people. They think what their pastor thinks. They buy the Bible version their spiritual leader has. They go where their friend tells them to go. They give the adult functions of life over to controlling people, sometimes to a ridiculous extent. Half of the problem is that too many people are willing to play God in other people's lives. Many spiritual leaders think that their job is to parent such "children" and keep them in check instead of to lead them into maturity under the lordship of Christ.

In the Christian world, too many people do not think for themselves. They do not question a teaching or doctrine; it is "right" because "so and so" says it is. If that person is a big-name leader, then it must be right.

Sixteenth-century reformer Martin Luther rebelled against this attitude, arguing for the priesthood of all believers. Luther felt that everyone could have their own relationship with God and could listen to teachers and decide what they believed instead of being told what they believed. "As for you, the anointing you received from him remains in you, and you do not need anyone to teach you. But as his anointing teaches you about all things and as that anointing is real, not counterfeit—just as it has taught you, remain in him" (1 John 2:27). Believers can rely on the Holy Spirit and the Word to interpret the interpreters and thus decide for themselves what they believe. John is not ruling out human teachers, as they are affirmed in the Bible, but all believers have the capacity to appreciate and appropriate God's truth.

No Equal Differences

People who live in a one-up and one-down world rarely consider differences acceptable. If someone believes or thinks something different, that someone is "wrong." There is no such thing as a difference of opinion or "agreeing to disagree."

These people also tend to treat differences in taste as being right or wrong. If their friends buy a certain car or move their kids to a certain school, they begin questioning themselves, "Do I have the right car?" or "Should I move my kids as well?" People who haven't grown up experience difference as a threat; if two people are doing two different things, someone must be doing the wrong thing.

This attitude can affect very small things such as what sale to go to, or what clothes to buy, or which pickleball paddle is "better." These people always ask, "Which is the better of the two?" instead of, "You like that one, and I like this one." The latter is the way two equal adults experience their differences.

These pharisaical minds have such a stringent list of what is "right doctrine" that they miss the real doctrine of "Love your neighbor as yourself." They are so concerned with determining how others are "wrong" that they can't love them. The Pharisees did this over and over again; they saw others as "less than" them, and therefore bad.

Black-and-White Thinking

People who can only see the world as black and white, right or wrong, are stuck in a pre-adult way of thinking. They are thinking like an eleven-year-old. They are unable to think in terms of gray; there are no tough moral dilemmas. Everything is simple. "If the rule says it, do it."

Jesus repeatedly ran into this sort of thinking with the Pharisees, and he tried to lead them past this rigidity to an adult position of love. I wish we all had a nickel for every time he heard the Pharisees ask, "Is it lawful for . . . ?" They were so preoccupied with the rules and right and wrong that they could not get to wisdom, truth, and love.

People who are stuck here adhere to rules that

have an "appearance of wisdom" (Colossians 2:23) but are worthless to bring about maturity. Rigorously obeying human-made rules instead of showing God-made love will always cause problems. This is why the adolescent passage of "breaking the rules" is so important.

Judgmentalism

Judgmental people fuse with the parental, legal position and look down on everyone else. They not only resist identifying with the acting-out adolescent inside, but they also judge it. "But the Pharisees and the teachers of the law who belonged to their sect complained to his disciples, 'Why do you eat and drink with tax collectors and sinners?' Jesus answered them, 'It is not the healthy who need a doctor, but the sick. I have not come to call the righteous, but sinners to repentance'" (Luke 5:30–32).

Judgmental people don't identify themselves as sinners; therefore, they aren't forgiven and can't become loving. Instead, they deny the "sinner within" and act like they are perfect and "above" sin (Matthew 23:27–29).

Anytime we look "down" on someone else, we have "seated [our]selves in the chair of Moses" (Matthew 23:2 NASB) above everyone else, and therefore have not identified with the sinner position within. The essence of the adolescent passage—the confession of the sinner within—puts us in a humble position under God instead of a proud position with people.

Anxiety Attacks

Both generalized and specific anxiety can be related to authority problems because anxious people fear disapproval externally as well as internally. Generalized anxiety signals something dangerous about to emerge into one's consciousness. People who suffer anxiety attacks often fear disapproval from the parental conscience.

Sam came into therapy for anxiety attacks. He suffered these attacks whenever he was dealing with a parent figure. When he was discussing a negotiation with a "father figure" in the law firm, for example, he became overwhelmed with anxiety.

Sam thought his problem was fear of authority, but in reality, he was afraid of his own strengths.

His feelings of equality were emerging and threatening the internal demand of his conscience to stay one-down to father figures.

As he gave himself permission to grow up and challenge these parent figures, his conscience gave him permission to be equal and aggressive in a good way. His anxiety disappeared, and his ability to close cases increased. Because he had conquered his fears of challenging authority figures, in a few years, his income quadrupled. He was afraid of being equal, not unable to be so.

Impulsiveness and Inhibition

Both license and inhibition can stem from authority problems. On the one hand, some people can be so angry at authority that they completely deny any rules or standards and live lawlessly. These people are often impulsive and do whatever they wish. These out-of-control adolescent adults have done away with authority, even God's.

On the other hand, legalists are so bound up with guilt, they aren't even aware of their impulses. These people are very shy and inhibited, and they often struggle with feelings of embarrassment. Their friends often say, "Let your hair down sometimes." Or in Solomon's words, "Do not be overrighteous, neither be overwise—why destroy yourself?" (Ecclesiastes 7:16). They don't feel free enough to enjoy life or their feelings.

Superiority

Superiority is the opposite of inferiority. Some people always find a way to see themselves as better than everyone else. It can look like narcissism, or idealism, but it is really one-upmanship. If someone has a superiority complex, they have exaggerated opinions of their own accomplishments and abilities. Consciously, an individual creates their own lifestyles to overcome feelings of inferiority.

Parenting Others

Some people who have never grown up think they know what others "should" do. They are unable to realize their own limited knowledge of a person's situation, as well as the person's responsibility or ability to deal with his or her own problems.

Counselors and teachers who in a controlling way directly tell others what to do fall into this category. They do not foster maturity in their clients, but rather make them dependent on them. These counselors try to justify their omnipotence by aligning themselves with the "authority of Scripture." But they often use the law like Pharisees, placing themselves in the "seat of Moses." They pay little attention to helping others learn the "more important matters of the law—justice, mercy and faithfulness" (Matthew 23:23). They like to dominate those "under" them.

You can spot parenting people by their overuse of the term "you should." Much of what they say to others has a parenting sound; others speak of feeling "crummy," or "guilty," or "convicted" after being with them. But the conviction is the type that makes people feel like prisoners instead of being the true conviction of God, which is tender and graceful.

Hate for Authority Figures

Some people never identify with authority; instead, they resist it either actively or passively. These adults are perpetual teenagers, never identifying with the adult position and always taking adolescent cracks at leaders.

Passive resisters constantly criticize people in authority, conveying a subtle feeling that they are superior to their superiors. They undermine the authority's decisions and wisdom and speak of them behind their back; they find the bad in every leader or pastor.

Active resisters are the rebellious "haters of authority" the Bible speaks about. These people openly resist any authority figure and generally rebel against authority of any kind, including God's.

The parable of the two sons (Matthew 21:28–32) illustrates these two positions. It was only the son who was aware of his rebellion who could repent and own it.

Depression

This depression stems from a "bad me," self-critical attitude. People who are criticized by their internal parent feel bad and guilty, which leads them to depression. They have not become free from parental structures. When these people get in touch with their anger at their critical parent and use this anger constructively to separate from that parent and become an adult, their one-down depression goes away, along with their anger, and they often find all sorts of creativity in its place.

Dependency

Some people actively avoid taking responsibility for themselves and find someone to parent them. They give executive power of their life to someone else. People who always need someone else to make decisions for them and to do things for them lack self-respect and usually are angry and resentful of the "parent" figures who are keeping them from growing up.

It is not unusual for people to marry out of dependency and then resent their partners for treating them like children. These people usually rebel either actively or passively to get an equal standing with their mate. Sometimes the person gets divorced to get their autonomy from the "parent spouse," acting out their adolescent rebellion toward their spouse and taking a household down with them.

Idealization of Authority

The perception that someone in authority is perfect presupposes a one-down position, because people who have identified with authority realize that authority figures are just like them, with warts and all. Idealized authority figures are not expected to have weaknesses and faults as well as strengths, even though the Scriptures tell us they will. "Every high priest . . . is able to deal gently with those who are ignorant and are going astray, since he himself is subject to weakness" (Hebrews 5:1–2).

People who idealize authority need to be reminded of the sins of David, Paul, Moses, and Peter, and shown that being an adult is not as scary as they think. They don't have to be perfect to be an adult. It is really only stepping up to a different kind of childhood, to being children of God (Galatians 4:4–5).

Idealization of Childhood

Because of their conflicts with becoming an adult, some people idealize childhood and see it as the only life worth living. They think that adulthood is full of drudgery and responsibility; it's boring. They avoid becoming adults and devalue it.

People who **idealize** authority need to be reminded of the SINS of David, Paul, Moses, and Peter, and shown that being an **adult** is not as SCARY as they think.

BARRIERS TO BECOMING AN ADULT

In the same way that other stages can be stagnated because of convictions about ourselves, others, and God, so can the stage of becoming an adult. These distortions need to be challenged and risked in new relationships other than the ones that they developed in, just like the other stages. Here are several.

Distorted Thinking
Our View of Ourselves

I am bad if they don't approve of me. That proves it.

I am less than others.

I must please others to be liked.

I am bad if I disagree.

My opinions are not as good.

I have no right to my opinions.

I must get permission from others to . . .

I am bad if I fail.

I shouldn't feel so sexual.

Sexual feelings are bad.

My plans will never succeed.

I should defer to their beliefs, even though I
disagree.

I need someone else to manage my life. I am not
capable enough.

If I differ, I am wrong.

I think they should . . .

I shouldn't let myself feel . . .

I am better than they are.

My group is the right group.

We really have the best theology.

Our ministry is the only real one.

I know what's best for them.

I know better than them.

I could never teach him or her anything.

Adulthood is out of my grasp.

Our View of Others

They are all disapproving and critical.

They are better than me.

They will like me better if I am compliant.

They think that I am wrong or bad for disagreeing.

Their opinions are always right.

They will think I am bad for failing.

They have no weaknesses.

They never fail like I do.

. . . is easy for them.

Their beliefs are better than mine.

They know what's best for me.

They never feel . . .

They know everything.

They are never this afraid, or mad, or sad, or . . .

They will hate me for standing up to them.

Our View of God

God likes for me to be passively nice to everyone.

God wants me to always defer to my authorities, never questioning.

God does not want me to run my own life. He wants my "leaders" to do that.

God disapproves of me when I fail, just as my parents disapproved.

God does not like me to be aggressive.

God does not like me to disagree with the pastor.

God does not allow me freedom to choose some of my own values. They are all prescribed in the Bible. There are no gray areas.

God thinks others are more (or less) important than me.

God wants me to adhere to a bunch of rules.

God likes discipline and sacrifice more than compassion, love, and relationship.

Our View of the World

Competition is bad; someone always gets hurt.

Disagreement is bad; someone always gets hurt.

Conflict is bad; someone always loses.

There is no such thing as a "win-win" relationship.

People who are people pleasers are liked better than people who say what they think.

Everything has a "right answer." Especially since we have the Bible.

There is a right and wrong way of seeing everything. Perspective makes no difference.

Flexibility is license and lawlessness.

Sexuality is evil.

There is a right and a wrong way to do everything.

It will never work.

These heartfelt but misguided convictions about self, others, God, and the world are barriers to becoming an adult. Some of them we probably learned in the family we grew up in; others are just a part of the preadult mind. In any event, they can only be overcome with work, risk, prayer, relationship, and practice.

CHAPTER 7

LEARNING TO BECOME A MATURE ADULT

Learning to become an adult is not an easy task. Perhaps becoming an adult while you're already living in an adult body is even harder. But it is a necessary step to take to get out from under the authority of others.

"I cannot make good choices," wrote theologian Thomas Merton, "unless I develop a mature and prudent conscience that gives me an accurate account of my motives, my intentions, and my moral acts. The word to be stressed here is *mature*. An infant, not having a conscience, is guided in its 'decisions' by the attitude of somebody else. The immature conscience is one that bases its judgments partly, or even entirely, on the way other people seem to be disposed toward its decisions. . . . Even when the immature conscience is not entirely dominated by people outside itself, it nevertheless acts only as a representative of some other conscience. The immature conscience is not its own master."[2] Here are some of the skills you will need to become your own master under God, to become a mature adult.

SKILLS FOR BECOMING AN ADULT

Reevaluate Beliefs

We need to reevaluate what we believe. The time for "inherited beliefs" has passed; it is time for an adult faith. We need to look into why we think what we think and why we believe what we believe. Is it because we really believe it, or because someone told us to believe it? We need to recognize what is a belief of "tradition" versus what is a real heartfelt conviction from God, his Word, and our own experience. This questioning period could last awhile. But, when we are through, we will have developed a mind of our own.

Disagree with Authority Figures

Be honest about your disagreements with others. Most people have disagreements with authority figures, but they are afraid to admit to themselves how strongly they disagree. And they are afraid to voice their disagreements. If you are in a group where you are not free to have a different opinion on gray issues, be careful. Your group may have cult-like qualities.

Allow yourself freedom of thought, and do not call yourself "bad" for your opinions. No one is right about everything, and we all go through periods of reshaping what we think on any topic. Speak your opinions and listen to the criticism. Speaking out may help you shape your views, or you may help shape others' views. Critique others' thoughts as well. Disagreement is healthy, and "iron sharpens iron" (Proverbs 27:17).

See Parents and Authority Figures Realistically

Knock parents and other authority figures off the pedestal you've put them on. See their weaknesses as well as their strengths. Look at the ways you disagree with what they believe and think. Since no two people agree on everything, search your life for anyone with whom you agree on everything, or who you think has it all together. You may be either unaware of how you disagree, or you may be a flatterer.

Confess the sins of your fathers and then forgive them. If you idealize your parents, you are fusing with their mistakes, and you may become like them. Disagree with bad patterns, call them sin, and be different from the generations that went before.

Think also about the spiritual "heroes" of the Bible and their frailties, as Hebrews points out. They were all human like us.

Make Your Own Decisions

If people in your life are telling you what to think, believe, do, or buy, start making those decisions yourself. You are an adult; learn to think and act for yourself. Who cares if someone disapproves of the purchase you make? It's your money, and how you spend it is between you and God.

Anyone who tells you "You should" buy this and not buy that, or read this and not read that, or attend this and not attend that, might be parenting you. Giving advice or feedback and confronting is good, but parenting other adults is bad. Avoid people who take away your freedom as redeemed and adopted sons and daughters of God and who want to become your parents.

Avoid PEOPLE who take away your **freedom** as redeemed and adopted sons and daughters of GOD and who want to become your **parents**.

Remember the words of Paul: "Formerly, when you did not know God, *you were slaves to those who by nature are not gods.* But now that you know God—or rather are known by God—how is it that you are turning back to those weak and miserable forces? Do you wish to be enslaved by them all over again?" (Galatians 4:8–9, italics mine).

These legalists, or parent figures, or pushers of rules are "no gods." Therefore, take their opinion as you would another adult; listen, but do not feel compelled to do what they ask. You have only one God. Listen to him.

Practice Disagreeing

If you struggle with these issues, you probably have no shortage of parental types in your life. You have great opportunities to practice what you could not do when you were growing up: disagree and not do what self-appointed human gods tell you to do.

Be aware of the times when someone is parenting you and say what you are thinking. You do not have to be mean or even confrontational. Just say, "Well, I see your point, but I look at it differently. I think . . ."

This is normal conversation, even though it may feel disrespectful or mean to you if you haven't tried it before. Learn to be equal with those who have assigned themselves as gods in your life, or to whom you have given this exalted position.

Deal with Your Sexuality

If you are prudish or embarrassed by sex, your parents may still be looking down their nose at your sexuality, or at least that's the way you are perceiving it. Work on reeducating yourself about the beauty of sex; desensitize yourself to the "no-no" attitude you have toward it. If you feel ashamed, you may still be in a preadolescent stage regarding sex.

Become familiar with your body and cherish it. You may need to talk with someone you trust in order to get over the "hush-hush" feelings about sex that come from childhood. "Children don't talk about sex," but adults can. Stop whispering!

In addition, become aware more and more of your sexual feelings. This normal adult thing happens around age thirteen. If you are repressing your feelings, you may be keeping other sorts of adult functions from developing as well. All these functions affect one another, and as your repression of your opinions lifts, so will repression of sexuality and creativity.

One client regained her sexual feelings by spending a few weeks becoming aware of her own opinions about her boss! Her repression of her thoughts about this female authority figure served to repress other adult functions as well. You can't repress just one aspect of yourself; it usually affects many areas.

Give Yourself Permission to Be Equal with Your Parents

Many authority problems have as their kernel the inability to assume the role held by the parent. You either dislike the way this parent functioned in the role, or you are afraid of taking the role over. In either instance, this is the role you were born to assume, the adult role. Look at the ways that your parent fulfilled this role. Appreciate where your parent succeeded and choose other role models for where he or she failed. This will help your transition from child to adult.

In addition, look at the ways that you fear usurping

their position. Many people fear going through the adolescent passage, for they do not want to dethrone their parent.

Recognize and Pursue Talents

To become an adult requires that you own and recognize the talents and gifts God has given you. You may be aware of some area that you are gifted in, and God has been telling you to develop it in some way, but you have been burying that talent in the ground.

To develop your expertise, you must take the talents God has given you and do something. This may mean to take a course, or get a mentor, or do some study, or whatever. But the important thing is that you are developing the talents. If you do not know what your talents are, ask God. He will tell you. Also, get some other people's insight. Often, we cannot see our strengths.

Practice

This is important to develop whatever skill and expertise you are considering. You can't learn to be an authority and have expertise in an area if you don't have the freedom to practice and learn. Give yourself permission to fail.

No one ever became an expert in any area without trial and error. Whether it's homemaking, basketball, business, personal finance, teaching, Bible exegesis, or child-rearing, it takes practice to develop a skill. Practicing is an important aspect of realizing independence and adulthood.

Go out there and fail, and then laugh it off and do it again. Learn to value process more than result. Internalize the substance of the task as well as the product. People who are only results oriented do not often enjoy their talents. Learn to enjoy them; you will be exercising them for a long time.

Recognize the Privileges of Adulthood

When people realize how much freedom their child position is costing them—freedom to develop as God intended without approval from other adults— the one-down position starts to look like prison. Remaining in a child position is safe because others do all the thinking for you; all you have to lose is your self-respect.

Go out there and fail, and then **laugh** it off and do it again. LEARN to value PROCESS more than **result**.

Adults have freedom to choose their own talents, values, beliefs, relationship with God, tastes, friends, and church. They also can express God-given aspects of themselves, such as feelings and sexuality, without inhibition and fear or need for approval from anyone else. They can be themselves. Like Paul says in Galatians 4:1, the child owns everything but is not free to use it. Adults are.

Discipline Yourself

Adults discipline themselves. Proverbs says to "Go to the ant, you sluggard; consider its ways and be wise! It *has no commander, no overseer or ruler*, yet it stores its provisions in summer and gathers its food at harvest" (6:6–8, italics mine). The key phrase here is "it has no commander, no overseer or ruler." In other words, the ant is not under another ant's authority, yet it takes responsibility for its tasks.

If you lacked discipline when growing up, you may need to learn discipline now. Get a good friend to hold you accountable in this area; agree on something you are going to be disciplined to do and have some built-in consequences if you don't. I once agreed to pay a friend a sum of money if I did not follow an exercise program. I needed the consequences to make me act.

Gain Authority Over Evil

The Bible commands us to "resist the devil, and he will flee from you" (James 4:7). Jesus also said that he had given us authority to command the evil spirits. The Word and the power of Jesus' name is enough for you to bind the forces of evil as they present themselves, and if you do not know how to do this, it is probably important at some point to learn about spiritual warfare. We are to take dominion over the evil one.

Submit to Others Out of Freedom

An important aspect of becoming an adult is to learn to submit to others in love, without an authority conflict. This includes government, spouses, friends, evil people, bosses, and God. When we submit in love, we are displaying our freedom; if we submit in compliance, it is not true submission. It's slavery (Romans 13:1; Ephesians 5:21; Matthew 5:39; 1 Peter 2:18–19; Hebrews 13:17; James 4:7). Submitting to others as God has ordained is identity-affirming.

Do Good Works

"For we are God's handiwork, created in Christ Jesus to do good works, which God prepared in advance for us to do" (Ephesians 2:10). You are God's handiwork; you are a prized possession he has created for a function. In the same way Adam was created to have dominion and exercise good works in the garden, you have been created for a purpose.

As you are working with God to find your talents and develop them, seek him for the good works you are to do. They do not have to be grandiose. Your good work could be being a link between God and a few of your neighbors, using your skills as a homemaker, or it could be using your academic skills to develop relationship with someone in your class. It could be donating some time to an orphanage or to a needy family. The point is this: You have some expertise and using it for good works will help you realize your adulthood.

If you are in a rebuilding time where God has set you aside to heal you and develop you, give him time to do this. Don't think you have to go save the world too quickly!

Become a "Pharisee Buster"

We all have remnants of legalistic thinking and remain under the tutor of parental approval. Try to find ways you may still be operating under the old system of gaining approval in order to be okay. Look for legalism that has crept into your faith and ways that you are being "made for the Sabbath" (Mark 2:27). Let go of the ways you are trying to earn approval; they can only eat away at your soul.

Appreciate Mystery and the Unknown

One of the hallmarks of people with authority problems is their inability to tolerate mystery and the unknown. They need an answer for everything, and everything has to be wrapped up in neat little packages. Jesus kept trying to shake the Pharisees out of this rigidity.

In many ways God is "unsearchable" (Romans 11:33–34). He is so awesome that the more we know him, the more we realize we don't know. This is where worship begins. It is his very transcendence that we worship. Begin to appreciate the things that you cannot figure out about him and let them be. This is why we call him "God." If you can know everything about him, then he is no longer God; you are. This is the most serious authority problem of all.

Worship his mystery. Get out of the black-and-white "we-have-all-the-answers" mentality that keeps God in a box. He is much greater than that.

Love and Appreciate People Who Are Different

People often see other people as not as good because they are still trying to be the better child. When you can appreciate other people who are different from you, you have stopped sibling rivalry—the childhood battle of trying to be the better child to win parental approval—and have begun to assume an equal stance with your adult brothers and sisters.

SARA

When Sara came to me, she was filled with anxiety. Dominated by older peers, fearful of disapproval, and sexually unfulfilled, she had spent her life fruitlessly trying to please others. Instead of enjoying an equal relationship with her husband and peers, she was always in the position of the subordinate.

The causes of Sara's problem came clear as she talked about her early family life. "My parents were very strict," she said. "They always wanted me to do my best. My mother had a very strong personality. She told me what to do and how to do it. But then when I did things the way she told me to, she would still find things to criticize. I could never do anything right for her."

Sara's mother had never allowed her to find out what sorts of things she liked to do and to practice them at her own pace. Nor had her mother seen failure as part of the normal road to achieving expertise. When Sara became a teenager and tried to broaden her interests, her mother grew worse, even trying to dictate the clubs and activities that Sara engaged in.

Meanwhile, Sara's father kept his distance. He did not contradict her mother's statements, nor did he give much approval of his own. In fact, he also criticized Sara when he felt she was not living up to her potential.

Sara became a Christian in college. There she joined a group of rigid Christians who lived by rules and regulations. Having learned from her parents how to comply, she did pretty much whatever the spiritual leaders asked. She never expressed her own thoughts or wishes, especially when she sensed that they would have disapproved of her.

When Sara got married, she continued to comply. She did everything possible to please her perfectionistic husband. As a result, she grew more and more out of touch with her own feelings and desires.

Because Sara had not been allowed to pursue her own talents and opinions, and because she had never openly disagreed with her mother, she was developmentally still a child. She was unable to have peer relationships with other adults because she had never assumed adulthood.

When Sara began to understand her background, she went to work on herself. She met regularly with friends who had similar problems. Rather than parenting each other, they gave each other feedback and support.

Then Sara went to work on her relationship with her parents. Since they lived nearby, she had ample opportunity to change her approach. Instead of trying to please her mother, she said things like, "I understand that you would do it that way, but I think I'll do it this way instead." For months, her mother could not handle this "disobedient" forty-year-old, but over time she realized that Sara was not going to live to please her anymore.

Sara began to voice her opinions and thoughts in other settings as well. In a couples' Bible study, she sometimes disagreed with the leader. She also began to choose clothes that were different from her "spiritual leader's" tastes. When the perfectionistic women around her tried to tell her what to do, she ignored them and went forward with what she thought was best for her. And gradually their power over her lessened. She saw them as imperfect humans, like herself. Even though they gave directions forcefully, she did not have to order her life as they wished.

She battled internal, as well as external, voices. She learned to talk back to her internal "parent" which drove her to perfection. And she learned to survive the anxiety of being "disobedient." Over time, the parental voices in her head were stilled, and she grew less anxious.

She also began to pursue her own talents and take risks to develop them. When she feared failure, she reminded herself that her parents were not perfect either, nor did they have power over her life. Soon it became easier for her to accept failure as a normal part of the learning process.

She also had to own up to the anger she felt deep inside toward all the parent figures who had controlled her. When she stopped blaming herself for their criticism, she saw the pride disguised behind their comments. As a result, she stopped bowing to their authority, and her anger dissipated.

Finally, her stance of equality with other adults affected her sexual relationship with her husband. She was more direct with him about what she liked and didn't like; she allowed herself to be less inhibited, worrying less about his disapproval. With her new power she forced him to be less demanding, and she herself became much more sexually responsive.

Growing up took quite a bit of time, prayer, and work, but in the end Sara won. Out of a forty-year-old little girl, God grew an adult.

CONCLUSION

Meaning, purpose, satisfaction, and fulfillment are fruits of the issues we've discussed. Meaning comes from love, which flows out of bonding. Purpose comes from direction and truth, which form boundaries. Satisfaction comes from having the less than perfect be "good enough" in the light of God's ideal, and fulfillment comes from the adult ability to exercise talents.

And last, "the greatest of these is love" (1 Corinthians 13:13). What I have written about is a model that can help us become functioning human beings. But if that is the final goal, we have sold ourselves short. We were made to love, and the fully functioning person is one who takes his bonded, separate, forgiving, adult self into a world and denies that self for the sake of others. We have seen how this does not mean being without a person inside; it means having such a full one that it can be imparted to others.

Work on your ability to attach to others so that you can have your empty heart filled. Work on setting boundaries so you can own your own life. Work on confessing and receiving forgiveness so you can develop your real personhood. Work on assuming adulthood so you can be an authority. Then, go out and give it to others. Remember, "Greater love has no one than this: to lay down one's life for one's friends" (John 15:13). God bless you.

REFLECTION QUESTIONS

BECOMING AN ADULT

You may need to redeem the past, evaluate the present, and be different in the immediate future before you can become an adult.

The Past

In terms of the past, your attitudes about authority came from somewhere. It is important to see where you got them so that you can actively disagree with their negative aspects and forgive the injury. This process will help get you out of conflict with the adult role so that you can assume it. We can't assume a role we hate.

1. Who was a good authority figure for me in the past? What did I appreciate about them? What kind of modeling do I want to emulate?

   _____

   _____

   _____

2. What negative aspects of authority figures do I disagree with and would like to be different from? Why did I not like these attributes and what sort of feelings did they create in me?

_____

_____

_____

_____

3. What are my parents' strengths and weaknesses? My other early authority figures'?

_____

_____

_____

4. How did they injure me and have I forgiven them? Why not? What is the block?

_____

_____

_____

_____

5. What authority figures did I falsely comply with after I was old enough not to do that? Why?

6. What was adolescence like? Have I entered adolescence yet? Why have I resisted becoming an adult and who helped me resist by playing God in my life?

7. What legalists have I succumbed to and what "rule-bound behavior"? Why?

8. What detrimental places and situations have I ended up in because I let a parent figure(s) run my life?

_____

_____

_____

9. What talents have I neglected developing? Why?

_____

_____

10. Where have I fused with the ideas of someone else without thinking for myself?

_____

_____

_____

_____

11. Who have I been afraid to disagree with in my life?

_____

_____

_____

_____

12. Have I come into my own sexual identity since ado-
    lescence, or am I still "hush-hush" about sex? Am I
    still repressed?

    _____

    _____

    _____

    _____

The Present

Take a prayerful inventory of the present and ask
God to show you what situations are currently hurting
you and keeping you from growing up.

1. With whom do I feel one-down right now? In what
   areas? Why? Is it a good one-down as in mentoring,
   or is it a bad one-down as in personhood?

   _____

   _____

   _____

   _____

   _____

2. Who am I trying to one-up? Why? In what ways am I playing God in their life?

_____

_____

_____

3. Who am I trying to please and get their approval? Why? Is it worth it? Has that pattern ever helped me?

_____

_____

_____

4. What talents and expertise am I not developing at present because of some sort of fear? What am I doing about the fear? Am I getting help? How can I step out in faith to develop that expertise and allow God to make me into an adult?

_____

_____

_____

5. What role or office am I resisting identifying with because of conflict? Why?

_____

_____

_____

_____

6. What authority roles in my life am I failing to submit to lovingly? (For example, my boss, the police, my board of elders, God, the IRS.) How can this be destructive?

_____

_____

_____

_____

7. With whom am I fusing currently in terms of thoughts and opinions and not stating my own? With whom am I afraid to disagree?

_____

_____

_____

_____

8. In what situations do I hide from my sexual feelings or thoughts? Why? Who is the parent figure there?

_____

_____

_____

9. What "spiritual" group do I act "nice" around? What group of friends are more adolescent? Why am I trying to please this "spiritual" group and then passively rebelling on the side? How is this practice keeping me a child? Which person am I most afraid of being judged by? Why?

_____

_____

_____

10. What doubts and wonderings do I have about God or theology that I am afraid to face and research on my own? What is keeping me from finding out what I believe?

_____

_____

_____

11. What current spiritual leaders do I disagree with? Am I afraid to say my thoughts?

_____

_____

_____

_____

12. How are my spouse or closest friends functioning as parent figures in the negative sense of the term?

_____

_____

_____

_____

The Future

1. What authority figure do I need to go and disagree with? When?

_____

_____

_____

_____

2. What person will I stop hiding from? When?

_____

_____

_____

3. What ideas will I stop fearing to voice and think about? When?

_____

_____

_____

4. Who will I begin to show my real thoughts to? When?

_____

_____

_____

5. How will I get in touch with my adult sexual role? When?

_____

_____

_____

6. What plans will I make to find and develop my expertise and be a good steward of my gifts? When?

7. What role will I do better at assuming authority over? When?

8. What person will I do better at assuming authority over? When?

9. Who will I stop "obeying" that I have no business obeying? How?

10. What siblings (real siblings or siblings in the Lord) will I stop treating as if they were my parents?

_____

_____

_____

11. What will I do the next time I hear "you should"?

_____

_____

_____

12. What am I going to do about my lack of discipline?

_____

_____

_____

NOTES

1. Richard Fry, "More adults now share their living space, driven in part by parents living with their adult children," Pew Research Center, January 31, 2018, https://www.pewresearch.org/fact -tank/2018/01/31/more-adults-now-share-their -living-space-driven-in-part-by-parents-living -with-their-adult-children/.

2. Thomas Merton, *No Man Is an Island* (New York: Harcourt, 1983), 27.

ABOUT THE AUTHOR

DR. HENRY CLOUD is a clinical psychologist, pastor to pastors, and *New York Times* bestselling author. His 45 books, including the iconic *Boundaries*, have sold more than twenty million copies worldwide. Throughout his storied career as a clinician, he started treatment centers, created breakthrough new models rooted in research, and has been a leading voice on issues of mental health and leadership on a global scale. Dr. Cloud lives in Los Angeles with his wife, Tori, and their two daughters, Olivia and Lucy.

PRAISE FOR DR. HENRY CLOUD'S
CHANGES THAT HEAL

Dr. Cloud highlights four essential ingredients to growth with such clarity that no reader will fail to benefit. Growing takes time, prayer, and hard work. This book will at least ease some of your growing pains.

ARCHIBALD D. HART, PhD, dean, professor
of psychology, Fuller Theological Seminary

People coming from dysfunctional homes are automatically afraid of being close to people. *Changes That Heal* is a powerful and insightful book about bonding and boundaries. It shows how to connect to other people so that we may become whole people in spite of our broken and lonely past.

JIM AND SALLY CONWAY, directors, Mid-Life
Dimensions; authors, *Adult Children of Legal and
Emotional Divorce* and *When a Mate Wants Out*

All of us seek to be future-oriented individuals, but we live with so much baggage from our past and our history. Here is a well-written, biblically sound, readily comprehensible book that releases us to not only anticipate but enjoy the remaining years God gives to us.

TED W. ENGSTROM, President Emeritus, World Vision

What a true blessing *Changes That Heal* has been to Jan and me! Everyone can benefit from the scriptural insight of this excellent book to bring the healing that is necessary for full maturity in our walk and relationship with God and with others.

DAVE DRAVECKY, former San Francisco Giant, author of *Comeback*

Of all the professionals I know, Henry Cloud understands and explains best why people develop emotional and relational problems and how they can solve them.

DR. PAUL MEIER, Minirth-Meier Clinic

(ISBN 9780310351788)

ALSO BY DR. HENRY CLOUD AND DR. JOHN TOWNSEND

Boundaries
Boundaries Workbook
Boundaries audio
Boundaries video curriculum
Boundaries in Dating
Boundaries in Dating Workbook
Boundaries in Dating audio
Boundaries in Dating curriculum
Boundaries in Marriage
Boundaries in Marriage Workbook
Boundaries in Marriage audio
Boundaries in Marriage curriculum
Boundaries with Kids
Boundaries with Kids Workbook
Boundaries with Kids audio
Boundaries with Kids curriculum

How People Grow
How People Grow Workbook
How People Grow audio
How to Have That Difficult Conversation

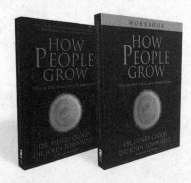

Making Small Groups Work
Making Small Groups Work audio

Safe People
Safe People Workbook

Our Mothers, Ourselves

*12 "Christian" Beliefs That
Can Drive You Crazy*

Raising Great Kids
Raising Great Kids for Parents of Preschoolers curriculum
Raising Great Kids Workbook for Parents of Preschoolers
Raising Great Kids Workbook for Parents of School-Age Children
Raising Great Kids Workbook for Parents of Teenagers
Raising Great Kids audio

GREAT BOOKS

ARE EVEN BETTER WHEN THEY'RE SHARED!

Help other readers find this one:

- Post a review at your favorite online bookseller

- Post a picture on a social media account and share why you enjoyed it

- Send a note to a friend who would also love it—or better yet, give them a copy

Thanks for reading!